Ideas
Teacher's Book

Ideas

Speaking and listening activities
for upper-intermediate students

Teacher's Book

Leo Jones

CAMBRIDGE
UNIVERSITY PRESS

PUBLISHED BY THE PRESS SYNDICATE OF THE UNIVERSITY OF CAMBRIDGE
The Pitt Building, Trumpington Street, Cambridge, United Kingdom

CAMBRIDGE UNIVERSITY PRESS
The Edinburgh Building, Cambridge CB2 2RU, UK   http://www.cup.cam.ac.uk
40 West 20th Street, New York, NY 10011–4211, USA   http://www.cup.org
10 Stamford Road, Oakleigh, Melbourne 3166, Australia
Ruiz de Alarcón 13, 28014 Madrid, Spain

First published 1984
Ninth printing 2000

Printed in the United Kingdom at the University Press, Cambridge

A catalogue for this book is available from the British Library

ISBN 0 521 27080 4   Student's Book
ISBN 0 521 27081 2   Teacher's Book
ISBN 0 521 24928 7   Set of 2 cassettes

Contents

Thanks

I should like to thank the teachers at the following institutions, where
the material in *Ideas* was piloted, for all their constructive suggestions
and criticisms and without whose help many improvements in the book
would not have been made: The British Institute, Madrid; The British
Institute, Rome; The British Institute, Florence; The British School,
Florence; The Cultura Inglesa, Sao Paulo; The Institute of English
Studies, Thessaloniki; The Newnham Language Centre, Cambridge;
The Studio School of English, Cambridge; The VHS Language Institute,
Nuremberg; and Pauline Bramall who used *Ideas* on in-company
courses in Germany. Thanks, too, to everyone who participated in
recording the listening exercises.

My sincere thanks also to Christine Cairns and Sue Gosling for all their
help and encouragement during the planning, writing and revising of
the material.

The author and publishers are grateful to the authors, publishers and
others who have given permission for the use of copyright material
identified in the text:
English Tourist Board for the extracts on pp. 40 and 41; A.P. Watt Ltd
for the extract on p. 95 from *The Dog Exercising Machine by*
Edward de Bono © The Cognitive Trust 1970.
The drawings on p. 16 are by Dave Parkins.

Introduction

Ideas is a book of speaking and listening activities for upper-intermediate students. There are 22 units, each based on a different topic and within each unit there are five to eight student-centred activities, designed to stimulate students to share their ideas, opinions and experiences with each other. The topics are the ones which most upper-intermediate students need and want to talk about in English, and the activities themselves are realistic, interesting and often challenging.

English is a language that is spoken not just in Britain, but all over the world – often as a means of communication between people who have no other language in common. The activities in this book don't attempt to prepare learners for 'life in Britain' but for using English as an international language.

Ideas covers the kind of listening and speaking skills tested in papers 4 and 5 of the revised Cambridge First Certificate exam (1984). It is also designed to be used as the oral/aural component of any course which concentrates mainly on reading and writing skills. And, of course, it can also be used on its own as an intensive 'refresher course' for learners who need to develop their fluency in English.

Activities

In the speaking activities in *Ideas*, students work together in pairs or in groups. The aim is to encourage students to exchange ideas and opinions with each other. In each activity students are given a purpose or task – and this makes the activities much more motivating and realistic than just 'answering questions' or 'having a discussion'. The tasks involve filling in charts, solving problems or finding out information.

Some of the activities in *Ideas* are called 'Communication activities'. Here learners are directed to separate sections at the back of the book, where each person is given different information and can't see the others' information. Their purpose then is to find out what their partners know and to tell them what they know. In this way an 'information gap' is created and bridged – and communication can take place.

In these activities each learner has a 'task' to perform and has to *use* the information he or she receives. Learners will find that they are strongly motivated by the desire to receive, offer and exchange information and by the realism and value of the tasks themselves.

The Teacher's Book provides a brief description of each communication activity with a 'route map' so that teachers have an overview of what will happen in the activity. There is also a complete index of the communication activities at the end of the Teacher's Book. (Some of the communication activities are used as 'clues' to help students who are having difficulty with a problem-solving exercise.)

Listening exercises

Each unit in *Ideas* has one or two listening exercises, the recording for which is on the cassettes. There is a clearly distinct 'before', 'during' and 'after' phase to each listening exercise. A full procedure for each phase is given in the notes for each unit, but basically the phases are like this:

1 Pre-listening   Learners find out their purpose in listening to the recording and any background information they may need. There is often also some preliminary discussion in which students talk together about their expectations and make predictions about what they are going to hear.

2 Listening   Usually learners need to hear the recording at least twice: once to get used to the voices on the tape and to try to get the gist of the text; and second to find out and note down the specific points of information required by the task. These tasks may involve drawing a diagram, filling in a chart or making notes, for example. Time should be allowed for a third listening if necessary.

3 After listening   Learners compare notes or answers with a partner and then discuss the topic, relating the information and ideas they have heard to their own knowledge and experience.

There are no 'comprehension questions' in the listening exercises: this is because in real life we don't ever have to answer such things. What we do have to do when we listen is gather information and then share it with others. This is the kind of skill the exercises in *Ideas* aim to foster. All the listening exercises therefore involve just as much talking as listening.

Working together

All of the activities in *Ideas* work best with learners working together in pairs or small groups. From time to time you may wish to vary this by getting the whole class to work together – not talking to 'the teacher' but to each other within the class.

The larger the class, the more these student-centred activities make sense, because:

- They give everyone a chance to speak.
- They allow real conversations to develop – not just pieces of language practice.
- They free learners from the fear of making mistakes or losing face.

In other words, when learners are working together in small groups, they are able to *communicate* with each other and are not just practising English or answering questions.

Of course, it's true that they are more likely to make mistakes (see below) but it's far better for a whole class to be talking fluently, with some mistakes, than for them all to be listening to the teacher and answering questions one at a time in turn.

Vocabulary and useful language

The teacher's notes for each unit give lists of essential and useful vocabulary connected with the topic of the unit. From time to time you may want to introduce *some* of this vocabulary before your class begins an activity. Usually, however, you may prefer to 'feed in' any words that seem to be needed by learners who are in difficulty and can't find the right words to describe an idea or object.

The vocabulary in these lists is drawn from the *Cambridge English Lexicon* but supplemented by further useful words which may be needed to discuss the topics in more depth. Words given in brackets are the American English equivalents of some of the British English words given in the lists.

In many of the activities some useful language is suggested – lists of phrases and expressions that learners can use while they are doing the activity. The purpose of the useful language is:

1 To provide language items which may help learners to participate more effectively in the activity. There is no need for them to memorise the expressions or try to 'work them into the conversation' – the phrases are there for *support* if and when needed.
2 To partially guide the conversation by showing learners what they might say at the beginning, in the middle and at the end of the activity.

The useful language sections do not contain exponents of any *one* particular function – each contains a range of expressions that students may find useful while participating in the activity.

Grammar and mistakes

Although accuracy is an important aspect of language learning and should never be ignored, it is far more important for learners to be able to *communicate* effectively. The activities in *Ideas* are 'task-orientated'

– learners are given a communicative task and their success (or failure) in performing this task will not necessarily depend on grammatical accuracy. These activities are related to the topic of each unit and require the use of a wide range of language skills. They provide essential 'fluency practice' – allowing learners to learn how to communicate by actually *using* English.

It is assumed that learners using *Ideas* will by this time have covered most of the basic grammar of English: there will still be some gaps in their knowledge, their memories may fail them sometimes and, of course, they will still make mistakes.

No learner should be (or even can be) corrected every time he or she makes a mistake. Indeed, if that happened, some students would become so 'mistake-conscious' that they would be afraid to speak at all! It must be realised that no one can learn a foreign language without making mistakes and that mistakes are actually an essential indicator of what learners still need to learn. On the basis of the mistakes you overhear, together with the questions you are asked, you can plan any remedial teaching your class may require. Two useful books to help you with this are *Notions in English* (CUP 1979) and *Use of English* (CUP 1984).

There is no point in attempting to 'revise the whole of English grammar' at an upper-intermediate level – not only might it be extremely boring, but it would involve wasting time on revising areas of grammar your learners are already familiar with. Specific difficulties can't be predicted. It's only when mistakes are made that you can see what the specific difficulties are – and *then* you should take action – but it is fruitless to try to anticipate all of these mistakes.

Written work

Although no written compositions are set in the Student's Book, there are a variety of list-making and note-taking tasks, particularly in the listening exercises. Here in the Teacher's Book, however, three suggestions for written work are given at the end of each unit. You may decide:

a) to select one of these yourself and explain to the class what they should do or discuss the topic with them, or
b) to allow your students to choose the written task they want to do after explaining the alternatives, or
c) to disregard these suggestions if your class already have enough written work to do, or if they aren't terribly interested in that particular unit.

In marking written work, try to maintain a balance between showing the need for writing to be reasonably accurate and recognising a student's desire to communicate fairly complex ideas. Clearly, if your students are soon to take an exam like the First Certificate, then accuracy is important and attention should be given to improving writing skills up to the level of the exam. The suggestions for written work are based on the kind of tasks set in the FCE exam. There is full coverage of the skills needed for all five papers of FCE in *Progress Towards First Certificate* (CUP 1983).

How to use *Ideas*

Teachers and students are expected to *select* the activities in each unit that seem most relevant and interesting to them. The 22 units cover a wide range of topics and although it is not essential to do the units in sequence, the later ones are more difficult than the earlier ones. It is recommended that Unit 1 is done first of all, because it is a kind of introduction to the methods and techniques used throughout the book. The teaching notes for Unit 1 are also more detailed than the notes for later units.

The teacher's notes for each unit begin with lists of useful vocabulary (see **Vocabulary and useful language** above), followed by advice on how to handle each activity. These notes become less detailed in later units, on the assumption that teachers will have become more accustomed to the techniques used by then. Finally, there are recommended writing tasks as a written follow-up to the unit (see **Written work** above). The teacher's notes also contain solutions to the problems or tasks set in the Student's Book and complete transcripts of the listening exercises.

Hopefully, each teacher will use *Ideas* in his or her own way, adapting the material to the needs of each different group of learners. The teacher's notes are intended as helpful prompts and not as rigid instructions laid down by the author! *Ideas* is designed to stimulate learners and teachers alike, not to control them.

One unit may take from $1\frac{1}{2}$ to 3 hours to work through, depending on:
    how difficult a class finds the activities,
    how much interest is generated,
    and how many of the activities are selected.

The teacher's role

The teacher has three main things to do while *Ideas* is being used:
1 To get things started – making sure everyone knows what they have to do and possesses the necessary vocabulary to do it.
2 To monitor the groups at work and decide when to stop the activity.

3 To lead a short follow-up discussion after each activity – answering any queries, pointing out any significant mistakes and then doing any remedial work necessary.

It is wise to rearrange groups and pairs frequently: this will help to keep the class feeling fresh and receptive to different people's ideas. It may, however, sometimes be necessary to make sure that the more dominant learners who might intimidate the less confident ones are kept together in the same group. Similarly, the shyest ones may prosper best talking to each other while they gain confidence. You may have to be constantly compromising between offering variety and playing safe when arranging pairs and groups. And sometimes old friends may work better together as a pair than enemies would!

While using *Ideas* your learners will be participating in enjoyable speaking and listening activities. Their enjoyment may tempt them to lapse into their mother tongue from time to time. The only solution to this (apart from imposing fines or even harsher punishments!) is to convince every member of the class that he or she has a share in your common aim: to improve their English. Indeed, one of the main aims of the material offered in *Ideas* is to foster a spirit of co-operation and friendship in the class – you are a team with a common purpose and each member of the team has his or her part to play in the success of the course.

Don't worry if the occasional activity seems to misfire or fails to 'take off' with a particular class. Open-ended exercises of this type are inherently unpredictable. Indeed, it was found during the piloting of *Ideas* that several activities which seemed to fall flat in one class went like a bomb in others. So, bear in mind the attitudes and prejudices of your class when you're selecting the activities you're going to do, and be prepared to 'sell' the idea of an activity to them if you believe it to be a particularly worthwhile one. Some activities are 'easier' than others, but this may not depend on the nature of the activity itself or the level of English required, so much as on the imaginations, opinions, experience, versatility and knowledge of the participants themselves. Above all, though, the activities are designed to be *enjoyable* – because students who are enjoying their course are still eager to continue improving their English and are receptive to new ideas.

1 You and me

This unit introduces the methods used throughout the book: students will be working in pairs or in groups sharing ideas, opinions and feelings – above all they will be working together. The emphasis in this unit is on the positive side of things – people's strong points, not their weak points; their achievements, not their failures. This doesn't mean that no one is allowed to mention things they hate or things which annoy them – students should be free to say what they feel like saying – but while doing this unit they should be looking at each other as team-mates, not as rivals.

Try to make sure during this unit that students change partners as much as possible for each of the activities. This will help them to get to know each other better. Note that most of the activities in this unit require students to work together in pairs: in other units the changes are rung and many activities will work best with groups of 3, 4 or more.

If possible, record as many students as you can on a portable cassette recorder so that you can analyse what gaps there are in their knowledge and what aspects of their spoken English need attention. You will, in any case, need a cassette recorder for the listening exercise and perhaps for the 'soft background music' suggested in part 4 of that activity. It might be a good idea to **make notes** on each student's spoken English, even if you don't record everyone. Your notes might take this form:

Student's name:

GRAMMAR POINTS:

VOCABULARY:

PRONUNCIATION POINTS:

There are no vocabulary lists for this unit – students should be encouraged to use the language they know already to express their ideas. There is however a vocabulary-building activity entitled 'Nice people' in this unit. Of course, if questions are asked and specific vocabulary items are requested, you should provide the words students need.

I HOPE YOU DON'T MIND MY ASKING

IN PAIRS

This activity is designed to help everyone to get to know each other better. The actual listening exercise (phases 1 to 3) should take less time than the rest of the activity (phases 4 and 5).

1 Before you play the recording, allow each pair time to discuss what answers they would themselves give to the questions in the table. One 'pair' may have to be a group of 3 if you have an odd number in the class.

2 Be prepared to play the recording at least twice through if your students are likely to find it difficult to understand people speaking at normal speed in English. The first time through they can just listen to get used to the voices and to try to get the gist of what the people are saying. The second time through they can make notes on what is said. These notes should just be a few words to help them to remember what was said.

Here are model answers to the listening task:

	First speaker	Second speaker	Third speaker
What do you enjoy most in life?	A nice meal	Reading a book in front of a fire	His work
What is your greatest ambition?	To go to Indonesia	To have enough money	To go on a safari in East Africa
What has been your greatest achievement?	Getting to Oxford	Having her daughter	Raising 3 daughters
Which person do you admire most?	Winston Churchill	Gandhi	His wife
Who do you get on with best of all?	His wife	Her daughter	His wife
What was the nicest thing that happened to you yesterday?	Daughter said he was wonderful	Went for a nice walk	Went for a drive in the country

3 Allow each pair time to compare their notes and then to assess the personality of each speaker.

4 For this part of the activity a cassette of some nice relaxing background music (orchestral or instrumental) might be useful. Play this music while the first pairs ask each other the questions from the list on the right of the page in the Student's Book. After 45 to 60 seconds stop the music and get everyone to change partners and,

when the music starts again, continue asking questions from the place
they had got to in the list. Keep on stopping the music and getting
everyone to change partners until they have all had a chance to talk to
most of their class-mates. The music will help to conceal any
embarrassing silences and act as a gentle cue for changing partners.

5 Make a clear signal (or stop the music again) and tell everyone to
change partners yet again. This time they should concentrate on
asking only the questions which they found most revealing or
interesting. Encourage them to give more detailed answers this time.

At the very end, find out what everyone thought of this activity – or
move straight on to the next page where students start to explore each
other's personalities in greater depth!

Transcript

Your students shouldn't expect to be able to understand every single
word that's spoken in this (or any other) listening text. All they should
aim to do is to pick out the main points of information, which in this
case are simply the answers to the questions that the interviewer asks.
The transcripts are given in the Teacher's Book only so that you, the
teacher, know what's going to be said and can 'handle' the exercise
more efficiently. Students do not need to see these transcripts, and in
fact it might be both time-consuming and confusing for them if they
did.

Interviewer:	Excuse me . . . er . . . could I ask you a few questions?
First passer-by:	Certainly, yes.
Interviewer:	Um . . . pl . . . could you tell me what you enjoy most in life?
First passer-by:	What I enjoy most in life? I think I enjoy . . . um . . . a nice meal.
Interviewer:	Mmm and what do you think's been your . . . or would be your greatest ambition?
First passer-by:	My greatest ambition would be to go to Indonesia and see the wonderful arts and dances and musics of that country.
Interviewer:	Oh yes, fascinating. Er . . . what's been your greatest achievement so far?
First passer-by:	My greatest achievement, well far be it from me to say but . . . um . . . I think that . . . er . . . I go back to the time that I got to Oxford. I was very very proud of . . . of . . . of finding myself at such a wonderful, hallowed . . . er . . . university of learning.
Interviewer:	Yes, I'm sure you were. What person do you admire most?
First passer-by:	Um . . . Winston Churchill.
Interviewer:	Mmm, and who do you get on with best of all?
First passer-by:	My wife.

Interviewer:	Oh . . . what was the nicest thing that happened to you yesterday?
First passer-by:	Yesterday . . . gosh, I must say my memory . . . isn't it awful . . . er . . . oh yes, my little girl came up to me first thing in the morning and she said, 'Daddy, you're the most wonderful person in the world.'
Interviewer:	Ha ha. Thank you very much.
First passer-by:	Thank you.
Interviewer:	Excuse me, could I ask you a few questions?
Second passer-by:	Oh . . . yes, all right.
Interviewer:	The first one is: What do you enjoy most in life?
Second passer-by:	Um . . . well, I . . . I'm sorry to be boring but . . . er . . . I really enjoy sitting in front of a fire and just reading by myself.
Interviewer:	That's lovely, isn't it? Yes and what's your greatest ambition?
Second passer-by:	Um . . . er . . . to have as much money as possible. I don't mean to be enormously rich but to be . . . have enough not to have to worry.
Interviewer:	Oh yes, and what do you think's been your greatest achievement?
Second passer-by:	Oh, having my daughter. I've got one little girl and it's her.
Interviewer:	Oh, lovely. Which person do you admire most?
Second passer-by:	Oh . . . er . . . um . . . well either something quite frivolous like . . . like an actor, like Laurence Olivier or . . . No, really somebody like . . . er . . . Mahatma Gandhi, I think.
Interviewer:	Oh yes. And who do you get on with best of all?
Second passer-by:	Oh, my daughter – she's awfully nice to me, ha ha.
Interviewer:	Ha ha, lovely. What was the nicest thing that happened to you yesterday?
Second passer-by:	Well . . . um . . . we went out for a very nice walk and . . . and saw a castle and it was just lovely, the whole day.
Interviewer:	Oh, it sounds super! Thank you very much.
Second passer-by:	Thank you.
Interviewer:	Excuse me . . . er . . . can I interrupt you for a moment?
Third passer-by:	Oh, yeah.
Interviewer:	Would you mind answering a few questions? The f . . . the first one is: What do you enjoy most in life?
Third passer-by:	Oh well, I think I enjoy my work most.
Interviewer:	Mmm . . . and what's your greatest ambition?
Third passer-by:	Greatest ambition. I think that would be to go on a safari in East Africa.
Interviewer:	Oh, that sounds wonderful. What's been your greatest achievement?
Third passer-by:	Well, I guess raising three daughters.
Interviewer:	Uhuh. Which person do you admire most?
Third passer-by:	Mmm . . . I'd better say my wife! Ha ha.
Interviewer:	And who do you get on with best of all?

Third passer-by:	Well, I . . . I'm sure: my wife.
Interviewer:	Again, your wife. And what was the nicest thing that happened to you yesterday?
Third passer-by:	Yesterday. . . . Oh yes, yesterday was Sunday and we went for . . . um . . . a drive out in the country and I think that was just wonderful.
Interviewer:	Thank you very much. Thank you, goodbye.
Third passer-by:	Bye.

(Time: 3 minutes 25 seconds)

WHAT KIND OF PERSON ARE YOU?

IN PAIRS

Whenever the recommended group size is given in these notes ('In pairs' or 'In groups of . . .') you may need to adjust the size to accommodate all of your students. For example, only sometimes does a class contain an even number of students, which means that there is often an odd man or woman out who needs to be made part of a group of 3 – or be *your* partner. In this unit, however, the latter course of action would be unwise, since you'll need all the time you can get to monitor what's going on and to make notes on your students' performance. So, whenever it says 'In pairs', this means that you can decide to have at least one group of 3 instead, with two members of the group sharing a role or sharing information.

If any of the questions in the questionnaire are embarrassing or worrying for anyone, point out the escape clause of [4] 'I'm not really sure'. Try to ensure that the activity ends on a positive note, not a negative one, by getting everyone to finish the activity with the one wish they would love to come true. This may make it necessary to leave out the middle of the activity.

Point out that the useful language included is there for support if they need it – to be used as required and not to be memorised and injected into every sentence!

MOODS

IN PAIRS

New pairs again here! At the end of the activity, the pairs could be combined into groups of 4 so that they can exchange their ideas on words to describe the girl's moods. The more personal questions at the end should perhaps be dealt with in pairs if the members of the class don't know each other very well yet.

NICE PEOPLE

IN PAIRS

Encourage students to ask each other the meaning of the words they don't know or to use a dictionary, rather than calling on you for help. Remind them that they are more likely to remember vocabulary they have found out for themselves than vocabulary you explain to them. This activity continues the theme of seeing people's qualities and not focussing on their faults.

WORKING TOGETHER

IN PAIRS

Draw everyone's attention to the purpose of this activity: working as a team to solve the problems by discussion, not working as two silent individuals. In fact, if a pair really can't make head or tail of one of the problems, they should ask another pair for a clue or even for a quick explanation. They shouldn't expect you to provide the right answers automatically – in fact even if only one pair has the right answer to a problem it's *they* who should tell everyone the solution, not you. Allow a reasonable amount of time for each problem to be worked on, before getting everyone to change partners and attempt the next. It doesn't matter if some pairs have already started the next problem before they change.
Here are the solutions to the problems that don't have immediately obvious answers:

2 (Make sure everyone notices the equipment piled on the roof of the Morris Minor!) The couple are in training for a two-year, 2,000-mile trip across Africa but have got stuck in the mud before leaving England.

3 If the sentences are numbered from 1 to 14, the correct sequence is:

10   8   5   14   3   7   4   9   12   2   6
11   13   1

5 a) They are husband and wife.
  b) The father is 40 and the son is 10.

WRITTEN WORK

1 Write a description of yourself, as if you were introducing yourself in a letter to a pen-friend.
2 Write your own CV (curriculum vitae) in English, giving details of your education and career.
3 What do you think are your own strengths and weaknesses? Write a paragraph on each.

2 It's a bargain!

This unit deals with talking about money, shopping and clothes.

Vocabulary

Some of the words below may come in handy when students are doing
the activities in this unit.
The words given in brackets ( ) are the **American English** equivalents
of some of the British English words given in the lists. Sometimes these
may not be **exactly** synonymous, or may not be used in quite the same
contexts. None of these words should be given out in list form to a class
– they are simply offered to you, the teacher, as a source of vocabulary
from which to select for your class's benefit.

shops
*department store, supermarket, corner shop (local store), stall, kiosk,
    market, arcade, shopping precinct, shopping centre (mall), jumble
    sale (rummage sale)*
*grocer, greengrocer, butcher, fishmonger, baker, tobacconist, florist,
    chemist/pharmacist (druggist), newsagent, bookseller*

shopping equipment
*cash register, checkout, counter, shop window, cash desk, trolley,
    shopping basket*

shopping
*cheap, a bargain, free, expensive, dear, pricey, valuable, brand-new,
    second-hand, reduced, in the sale*

money
*small change, change, cash, credit card, cheque, coin, note (bill),
    pound/quid, five pounds/fiver, £1000/grand, (5 cents/nickel, 10
    cents/dime, 25 cents/quarter, dollar/buck), exchange rate*

spending money
*TO . . . change, borrow, lend (loan), hire/rent (rent), pay in cash, pay
    by credit card (charge), pay by cheque, spend money on, buy
    something, pay for something, cost, be worth, make a profit/loss,
    break even, be rich/well off, be poor/broke, be in debt, go
    bankrupt/broke*

clothes
suit, trousers (slacks), dress, shorts, jeans
pants/briefs (shorts), panties, vest (undershirt), petticoat/slip, bra,
  tights (panti-hose), stockings, socks
pullover/sweater/jersey/jumper, V-neck, polo neck (turtleneck), round
  neck, cardigan, shawl
shirt, blouse, tie (necktie), bow tie, scarf
nightie, pyjamas (pajamas), dressing gown (robe)
shoes, boots, wellingtons, sandals, slippers
sleeve, cuff, collar, seam, stitching, hem, buckle, zip (zipper), belt
hat, cap, beret, hood, veil

wearing clothes
TO . . . put on, have on, wear, take off, suit, fit, try on

materials
cotton, wool, leather, suede, elastic, denim, canvas, cord, silk, velvet,
  satin, tweed, synthetic: nylon, polyester, acrylic
striped, flowery, patterned, plain

colours (colors)
yellow, gold, lemon; purple, violet; red, maroon, crimson, pink, orange;
  blue, navy; brown, tan, fawn, khaki, beige, chestnut; grey, black;
  green, olive
dark, light, bright, yellowish/bluish, etc.

IMPECCABLE STYLE

IN GROUPS OF 3 OR 4

Some other advertisements showing current fashions would be helpful
for students to comment on, too. Cut a few large ones out of English or
American magazines and show them to the class.

How much time does everyone spend shopping every week? What do
they enjoy and dislike about going shopping?

NEW CLOTHES 🔲

IN PAIRS

Here are some model sketches. Your students will need to hear the recording *several* times to get the details.

If appropriate, students could also describe their own 'national costumes' at the end of the activity.
(The interview with the *first* shopper is an example which shows students how to do the exercise.)

Transcript

Interviewer:	Excuse me, would you tell me what you've just bought?
First shopper:	Oh, er . . . all right, I've . . . er . . . just bought a pair of . . . er . . . brown jeans and a . . . and a red and blue striped sweatshirt. And it's got a big number one on the front and the . . . and the words 'All Stars' are on the back. Yeah, they're nice. I didn't buy them to go together, mind, you know they. . . .
Interviewer:	Not an ensemble?
First shopper:	No, no, they're just a couple of things I. . . .
Interviewer:	Right, thank you, thank you.
First shopper:	Lovely. Bye-bye.
Interviewer:	Bye-bye. . . . Excuse me! Excuse me, would you . . . er . . . tell me what you've just bought in this shop?
Second shopper:	Oh . . . um . . . well, I've bought . . . um . . . a long-sleeved dress with a high neck . . . um . . . not very short . . . um . . . the hem's just below the knee. It's black . . . er . . . but there are small red and green flowers all over it.
Interviewer:	Has it got a belt?
Second shopper:	Yes, it's got . . . um . . . a narrow belt . . . um . . . made of the same material. It ties at the side, like.
Interviewer:	Have you bought anything else?
Second shopper:	No, that's all.
Interviewer:	That's all, right. Thank you very much.
Second shopper:	I haven't bought anything else.
Interviewer:	Yes, OK, goodbye. . . . Oh, excuse me! Excuse me.
Third shopper:	Yeah.
Interviewer:	Er . . . er . . . could you describe . . . could you . . . could you tell me what you've bought from the shop?
Third shopper:	Is this the telly?
Interviewer:	No, it's not a telly, I'm sorry, it's . . . er . . . market research. Would you mind?
Third shopper:	Oh, well, I didn't buy anything in the shop. There was nothing I liked.
Interviewer:	Oh, I see.
Third shopper:	Nothing better than what I've got on now.
Interviewer:	Oh, well describe . . . well, what what have you got on? Let's see.
Third shopper:	Well, plain black T-shirt, blue jeans held up with a thick . . . er . . . brown leather belt, a large gold-colour buckle. Oh, and I've got of course my silver chain round my neck with a medallion on.
Interviewer:	I see. Thank you very much. Thank you, OK.
Third shopper:	That all right?
Interviewer:	Yes, that's fine. I don't need anything more. . . . Oh excuse me! You . . . er . . . yes, you've bought something?
Fourth shopper:	Yes.

Interviewer:	Oh . . . er . . . could . . . could you tell me what it is?
Fourth shopper:	Oh, well, I love all white. So, I've bought white cotton jeans . . . um . . . a white blouse with short sleeves and white canvas shoes.
Interviewer:	Oh, super.
Fourth shopper:	And I've also got a leather shoulder bag. But that's not white, no, that's brown.
Interviewer:	That's brown. Lovely. Thank you very much. Thank you. . . . Excuse me, sir!
Fifth shopper:	Yes.
Interviewer:	Yes, I . . . I'm doing some market research. Would you mind telling me what you've bought in your. . . .
Fifth shopper:	No, not at all. I've just bought a new suit, actually, for my work.
Interviewer:	Uhuh.
Fifth shopper:	Um . . . basically . . . a . . . a grey suit. But um . . . if you have a little look here, you can see that it has green and blue stripes, too. Rather . . . rather nice, I feel. . . .
Interviewer:	Very nice.
Fifth shopper:	The trousers . . . trousers here are fairly narrow.
Interviewer:	Yes.
Fifth shopper:	The jacket is a . . . is single-breasted with a . . . with a narrow collar. And it has two side pockets and a breast pocket. The waistcoat is a normal sort of waistcoat really. And well, I personally think the whole suit is sort of . . . I don't know, traditional sort of style.
Interviewer:	Very smart.
Fifth shopper:	Well, it'll suit my sort of . . . er . . . work anyway. Thank you so much for saying so.
Interviewer:	Thank you very much.
Fifth shopper:	Goodbye to you.
Interviewer:	Thank you, goodbye. . . . Oh, excuse me!
Sixth shopper:	Yes?
Interviewer:	Er . . . have you just bought something at the shop?
Sixth shopper:	Yeah, I've just bought a summer outfit . . . um . . . very colourful. A T-shirt in light blue, red and green stripes. Um . . . yellow cotton jeans, navy blue shoes and a straw sun hat with a wide brim.
Interviewer:	Er . . . that's all?
Sixth shopper:	Yeah, that's all.
Interviewer:	Oh, that's lovely. Thank you, thank you very much, goodbye.
Sixth shopper:	OK, bye.
Interviewer:	Yes, bye.

(Time: 2 minutes 50 seconds)

I'M LOOKING FOR A . . .

IN TWO GROUPS

In this activity students are playing the roles of shopkeepers and customers. The shopkeepers can remain in their places and 'set up shop' there, while the customers go from shop to shop trying to find the articles they require. After some time the roles are reversed – give a signal if this doesn't happen by itself.

Perhaps encourage everyone to bargain and even, after much lack of success in finding the desired article, to give up and try to find another article.

In a very small class of less than about 10 it may be necessary to eliminate some of the items in the list to make the activity work.

THE HIGH STREET

IN PAIRS OR GROUPS OF 3

Before you play the recording allow everyone a little time to make some guesses and perhaps exchange some 'knowledge of British life'.

According to the interviews the correct answers are as follows. Note, however, that there are branches of some of the stores which may stock a different range of goods to the ones referred to in the interviews.

C & A: clothes
W.H. Smith: books, records and stationery
Habitat: furniture (and household goods)
Boots: medicines (and household goods)
J. Sainsbury: food
Dixons: photographic and audio equipment
Debenhams: most things except food
British Home Stores: clothes, food and household goods
Marks and Spencer: clothes (and food)
Safeway: food
Curry's: electrical goods
Tesco: food
Dolcis: shoes

Transcript

Reporter:	Hallo. I've got a crowd of shoppers around me this afternoon and I'm going to find out what they've been buying. Excuse me . . . er . . . could you tell me what shop that you've been to this afternoon?
Shopper 1:	Er . . . Dolcis. Yes . . . um . . . and Smith's. I bought some shoes in Dolcis and a record in Smith's.
Reporter:	Fine, thank you. And you?
Shopper 2:	Yes, I've been to Tesco, actually, and I've bought some food.
Reporter:	Great. And what about you, sir?
Shopper 3:	Oh . . . I've been to Curry's, you know, the electrical people and I've bought myself a new electric shaver.
Reporter:	Great. And what about you, madam?
Shopper 4:	Er . . . well, I bought all this food in . . . er . . . Sainsbury's.
Reporter:	Mmm. And you?
Shopper 5:	Yes, I bought um . . . a pullover from Marks and Spencer's and . . . um . . . I also went to Debenhams and bought a tennis racket.
Reporter:	Sir, what have you got?
Shopper 6:	Er . . . a lamp, some socks and some apples from British Home Stores.
Reporter:	Fine. And what about you?
Shopper 7:	Er . . . some tights and some make-up and a record, all from Debenhams.
Reporter:	Fine. And anyone else? Yes!
Shopper 8:	Yeah, I've bought a jacket from C & A and some . . . er . . . writing paper from Smith's.
Reporter:	Great.
Shopper 9:	Yeah, I've . . . I've . . . er . . . what shall I speak now?
Reporter:	Yes.
Shopper 9:	I've got my . . . I've got my food for the week from Safeway's.
Reporter:	Great. And you?
Shopper 10:	Well, I haven't bought anything actually, I've . . . we've been looking at cameras and, er . . . you know, hi-fi equipment in Dixons.
Reporter:	Great. What about you, madam?
Shopper 11:	Well, actually, I've got an awful cough and I'm just going to go to . . . um . . . Boots for some cough medicine.
Reporter:	OK. Now, a couple here.
Shopper 12:	Well, I . . . do you want to speak or shall I . . . .?
Shopper 13:	Well. . . .
Shopper 12:	We've been. . . .
Shopper 13:	We're going to look at some furniture in . . . er . . . in . . . um . . . Habitat.
Shopper 12:	And then perhaps we're going to go to Debenhams.
Shopper 13:	Debenhams, yes.
Reporter:	Great. Thank you very much indeed.

(Time: 1 minute 40 seconds)

YOU KNOW WHAT I'D LIKE?

IN PAIRS

Make it clear that they shouldn't try to think of things that are marginally cheaper in the UK or USA – that's just penny-pinching. They should think of things that are in some way typical of each country. If your students have no knowledge of Britain or the USA, get them to talk about other countries they do know something about.

A LITTLE SOMETHING

IN GROUPS OF 4 OR 5

Each group can only give *one* present to each of the people in the other groups. At the end, when the gifts are announced to the assembled class, find out the reasons for the choices made – unless these are obvious!

WRITTEN WORK

1 Do you enjoy shopping? Explain *either* what you like about it *or* what you hate about it.
2 Describe a well-known shop or store in your country – one you think a foreign visitor should go to.
3 Imagine that a friend of yours is living in a foreign country. Write a letter asking your friend to bring you back a number of things on his or her next trip home.

3 Lovely day!

This unit deals with talking about the weather and different climates.

Vocabulary

climate
*dry/rainy season, winter, summer, autumn (fall), temperature,
thermometer, rainfall*

weather
*snow, sleet, slush, sunshine, shower, drizzle, downpour, gale, breeze,
hurricane, fog, frost, hail, mist, ice, storm, thunder, lightning,
thunderstorm, gust of wind, dew, haze, snowstorm, blizzard,
snowdrift*

weather
*wet, dry, damp, windy, calm, hot, warm, stuffy, close, humid, cool,
chilly, freezing, mild, fine, bright, fair, overcast, dull*
*It's going to . . . snow, pour with rain, freeze, warm up, cool down,
brighten up*

ways of starting a conversation by mentioning the weather
Not very nice today, is it?   *No, it's not.*
Lovely day, isn't it?   *Mmm, yes, it certainly is.*

IN THE SNOW

IN PAIRS

After beginning the discussion in pairs, the groups could be expanded
into fours. Make sure everyone has a chance to reminisce about their
own experiences of extreme weather conditions.

Encourage them to cast their minds back and remember how they felt on
the coldest, hottest, wettest and windiest days they remember. What is
everyone's idea of 'perfect' weather?

IT ALL DEPENDS ON THE WEATHER

IN GROUPS OF 3 OR 4

Try to arrange groups of mixed nationalities in a multilingual class. In a monolingual class, each group could consider a different season for the imaginary foreign friend's visit.

YOUR HOLIDAY WEATHER

IN PAIRS

Before playing the cassette, give each pair time to discuss what kind of weather they might expect to find in each place shown on the map. If they are unfamiliar with European geography, get them to identify the countries listed on the left of the map by drawing lines between the names of the countries and the appropriate places on the map. This preliminary work will help them to 'tune in' to the topic of the broadcast and to build up some expectations as to its content.

Play the cassette at least twice and if necessary reassure your students that they don't need to understand every word the weatherman says, just the relevant information on temperatures and kinds of weather.

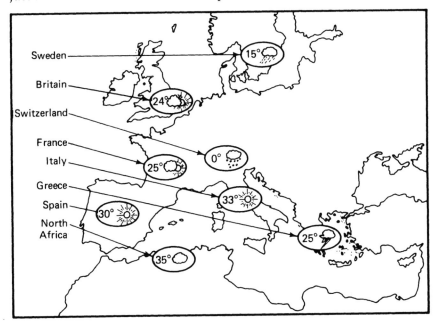

Transcript

Announcer: . . . and now over to the weather centre where Harry Spicer is going to tell you all about your holiday weather.

Weatherman: Thank you, Jenny. Yes, this is the first really busy holiday weekend coming up and I'll begin with some information about the weather in Europe and around the Mediterranean. Starting off, though, with England and Wales to give you an idea of the kind of weather those of us who are staying at home are going to get. Well, quite a warm day tomorrow with temperatures around 24° mark and . . . er . . . hazy sunshine in most places. On the Continent, rather a different picture. In Scandinavia, Sweden can expect quite a cold day with temperatures of 15° and some quite heavy rain in the east. Norway and Denmark less cold but still wet most of the day. In France, the high pressure may give rise to a shower here and there, especially in the west but over most of the country there'll be hazy sunshine and temperatures very similar to those in England and Wales, around 25° Centigrade. Spain should be warm and dry with temperatures up to 30° and a lot of sunshine and a similar picture in Italy, where it may get even hotter and temperatures around 33° can be expected tomorrow. The very hot weather recently in the Eastern Mediterranean has been hitting the headlines but this seems to be over now and if you're going to Greece, you can expect some very heavy thunderstorms in the afternoon and evening: it's going to be quite a lot cooler than of late . . . er . . . temperatures round about 25° here tomorrow. Morocco and the rest of the southern Mediterranean is going to be extremely hot around 35° but here it may well be quite cloudy during the day with skies not clearing until nightfall. Finally a big contrast in the Alps, where snow has been falling over the mountains in Switzerland and Austria since this morning. Here above 2000 metres it'll be around freezing most of the day tomorrow and there'll be more snow, some of it quite heavy. So if you're headed in that direction, perhaps you'd better take your winter clothes. That's all from me for now and . . . er . . . now back to Jenny.

(Time: 2 minutes 20 seconds)

OH TO BE IN ENGLAND ▐▌▌

IN GROUPS OF 4 OR 5

In this activity each group begins by speculating on the climate in each of the places on the map. When they have made their guesses, they can get more information in the form of statistics in the communication activities – half the group looks at 14, while the other half looks at 27. The idea is then to exchange information – but not just to read out the numbers, of course, rather to interpret the figures given and compare them with their original guesses.

USEFUL IN THE RAIN?

IN GROUPS OF 3 OR 4

It may be necessary to help an unimaginative group by giving some examples of what is required. Perhaps consider as a class what possible uses they can think of for *a pencil*: writing, pointing at things, beating out a rhythm, cleaning the ears, etc.
A small prize might be offered to the team that comes up with the most ideas. A very imaginative class might need to be restricted to thinking up uses for half of the objects illustrated.

HELP!

IN GROUPS OF 4 OR 5

Answer: One boy stays on the hill, the other rows to the house and changes places with one of the adults. The adult rows alone to the hill and gets out of the boat. The boy on the hill gets in, rows to the house, picks up the other boy and they go back together to the hill. Then one of the boys rows back to the house, gets out of the boat and one of the remaining adults gets in and rows to the hill. . . .
Finally, the boy on the hill rows across to the house to pick up the other boy and bring him back to the hill safely – or they can both row off into the sunset!

If one or more groups manage to solve the problem fairly quickly, get them to explain their solution to another group – the task in this activity should involve both working together *and* explaining the process.

WRITTEN WORK

1   Write a narrative beginning with a sentence about the weather and ending with another sentence about the weather.
2   Imagine that a friend from a country with a totally different climate from yours is soon coming to stay with you in your country. Write a letter explaining to your friend what to expect when he or she arrives.
3   Write one very long sentence explaining all the uses you can think of for one of the objects shown in 'Useful in the rain?' on page 13.

4   Keep in touch

This unit deals with talking about telecommunications and with making and receiving telephone calls.

Vocabulary

writing
pen, pencil, biro, ballpoint, typewriter, teleprinter (teletypewriter)
airmail, surface mail, express mail, post code (zip code)
letter, memo, note, telex, telegram/cable (wire), postcard, air letter
postman (mailman), post office clerk, post office, postbox (mailbox)

telephones
receiver, dial, hook, push-button dial, phone box/call box, phone
book/directory, an ex-directory number (unlisted number),
switchboard, exchange (central), local call, long-distance call,
transferred charge call (collect call), personal call (person to person)
operator, telephonist, caller, subscriber

telephoning
TO . . . ring (call), phone, hold on, be through (be connected), put
someone through, be finished (be through), be engaged (busy), be out
of order, be ringing

INFORMATION ON TAP

IN GROUPS OF 3

In Britain there are several similar systems which can show information on a TV screen: Teletext (Ceefax and Oracle), Prestel (150,000 pages of information supplied via telephone lines) and private computer information banks.
Does everyone think Teletext is just a gimmick, or will we all use such a system one day?

CAN I TAKE A MESSAGE?

IN PAIRS TO BEGIN WITH

The first call on the recording should be played as an example – it's Mary Roberts, as shown in the Student's Book. Then play the next calls, pausing the cassette between each one. After everyone has noted down the other messages and compared notes with a partner, it may be necessary to play the recording through again to clear up any confusing points – however, there is no need for everyone to understand every word that was said, of course.

The following messages contain the important information given by each of the callers:

> <u>Bill</u>: Henry Griffiths called – Can you meet him at 3.30 not 2.30 tomorrow? If you can't, phone him any time tonight on 01 489 3572.
>
> Linda: Anne Bridge called – her kids have measles. Please phone her at breakfast time – 444 0466.
>
> <u>Linda</u>: Message from George Harris: everything OK for Saturday. Please be there at 10, doors open at 11.
>
> <u>Bill</u> PRIVATE! Message from one of your colleagues at work: Mr. Goodman asking awkward questions. Make sure you arrive early tomorrow and have good excuse ready for leaving early today! Sorry but didn't get the caller's name – a woman.

John (the baby-sitter): Hallo, 237561.
Mary: Oh, hallo. Er . . . could I speak to Bill?
John: Ah, afraid he's not here at the moment. Could I take a
    message for him?
Mary: Um, yes . . . er . . . um . . . yeah, would you ask him to phone
    me tonight before 11, if he gets back before then – I go to bed
    11 . . . at 11 . . . yes? Er . . . or tomorrow morning . . . er . . .
    before I leave for work . . . I . . . I leave the house about 9
    o'clock. OK?
John: Right, yeah.
Mary: My number is 251 . . . 192.
John: Right and you, oh . . . what's your name?
Mary: Oh, oh, sorry . . . Mary . . . Mary Roberts.
John: Mary Roberts.
Mary: Right thank you, thank you very much.
John: Fine, I'll give him the message. Goodbye.
Mary: Bye.

John: Hallo. 237561.
Henry: Oh, Henry Griffiths here. Can I speak to Bill, please?
John: Ah, afraid Bill's not in, can I take a message for him?
Henry: Oh . . . um . . . yes . . . look I've . . . I've arranged to meet him
    tomorrow afternoon at the station. . . .
John: Yeah.
Henry: At half past two. Um . . . look, I can't make it at that . . . as
    early as that now. Can you give him a . . . a . . . message?
John: Er . . . yes.
Henry: I want to . . . want to change the time of the meeting to 3.30
    please, instead of 2.30.
John: Yeah.
Henry: All right? Now, look, if this isn't possible, can you get Bill to
    phone back at any time tonight.
John: Yes, what . . . what's your number?
Henry: It doesn't matter how late it is, just get him to ring back.
John: What's your number?
Henry: Er . . . my number is 489 – that's 01 at the beginning – 489
    3572. Now look, if I don't . . . if I don't hear from Bill, I'll
    assume 3.30's all right tomorrow.
John: 3.30 at the station. What's your name again?
Henry: Henry Griffiths.
John: Fine, I'll give him the message.
Henry: Thanks so much. Bye-bye.
John: Goodbye.

John: Hallo. 237561.
Anne: Oh . . . um . . . is . . . is Linda there?

John: Er . . . no, I'm afraid she's out at the moment.
Anne: Oh Lord . . . um . . . well, look . . . um . . . this is Anne Bridge
           speaking . . . um . . . my. . . .
John: Oh, hang on, I haven't got a pencil, hang on just a second . . .
           right, Anne Bridge, yeah.
Anne: Yes, my children were going to come to Linda's house
           tomorrow morning but . . . er . . . my eldest has got
           measles. . . .
John: Yeah.
Anne: So I think we'd better call it off . . . um. . . .
John: Right, so you're not coming tomorrow?
Anne: Well, well, unless Tommy and Jenny have both had measles
           already and then . . . and then it'll be all right. But I don't
           know. Um . . . oh, look . . . um . . . could you get Linda to call
           me at breakfast time?
John: Yeah.
Anne: Thanks.
John: Oh . . . what's your . . . what's your number?
Anne: Um . . . 444. . . .
John: Yeah.
Anne: 0456.
John: 0456.
Anne: Yeah.
John: Right. I'll give her the message as soon as I see her.
Anne: Oh, thanks a lot, sorry to trouble you. Bye.
John: That's all right. Bye-bye.

John: Hallo. 237561 here.
George: Hallo . . . hallo, do you think I could speak to Linda?
John: Er . . . afraid she's out at the moment. Can I take a message
           for her?
George: Ah, now, it's about the arrangements for Saturday.
John: Yes.
George: Saturday, no? Um . . . this is awfully difficult, now, well
           perhaps you could tell her that everything's all right. We've
           booked the hall, and they . . . all the helpers have been
           contacted and they . . . and they've all agreed to turn up. So
           . . . so if all's well . . . I . . . I'll see her there at 10 o'clock, all
           right? And doors open at 11. Could you say that? Should be
           there at 10 o'clock because the doors open at 11.
John: Yeah. Who actually are you?
George: I . . . George Harris.
John: Yeah. Has she got your number?
George: She has, thank you so much.
John: Fine. Do you want to give it to me just in case?
George: No, it's all right I think, it's perfectly all right, that.
John: Fine. I'll give her the message, then. Goodbye.
George: Goodbye to you.

John: Hallo. 237561.
Woman: Oh, hallo, could I speak to Bill, please?
John: Er . . . afraid Bill's not in at the moment.
Woman: Oh . . . um . . . oh . . . er . . . who are you?
John: It's John, the baby-sitter.
Woman: Oh . . . um . . . well . . . will you be speaking to Bill tonight?
John: Er . . . possibly.
Woman: Yes, well, could . . . could you give him a message, but it's
             quite private. I mean his wife shouldn't know. Right? Yeah,
             you see, Bill left . . . he left work early this afternoon, you see,
             about 2, actually.
John: Yeah.
Woman: And Mr Goodman, he's our boss, he noticed and he's been asking
             me where he went . . . well . . . I mean, I know where he went and
             . . . um . . . but I'm sure his wife doesn't know and . . . and the boss
             doesn't know. So . . . would you just tell Bill that . . . er . . . when he
             comes in tomorrow morning, he ought to come in early and he
             ought to have a really good idea of, you know, where he's been
             and why he had to leave early . . . um . . . today. You see what I mean?
John: Right, yeah. But I mustn't tell his wife?
Woman: No, no, don't tell his wife, heavens, right.
John: Right.
Woman: Er . . . OK?
John: Fine. I've got that.
Woman: Thanks, thanks a lot, you . . . you'll make sure . . . um . . . his
             wife doesn't hear, won't you?
John: Yes, I'll give him the message.
Woman: Yeah, great, thanks a lot. Bye.
John: Bye.

(Time: 4 minutes 55 seconds)

ON THE PHONE 📺

IN PAIRS

Student A begins at communication activity 12 and goes on to 43
afterwards.
Student B begins at 56 and goes on to 38 afterwards.
The first 'phone conversation' is about a bike advertised for sale, the
second about some concert tickets advertised for sale. To make the
conversations more realistic, arrange the seating so that the pairs aren't
looking at each other during their 'phone conversations' – they should
sit back to back if possible.
If you have an extra student, with no partner, join up with him or her
yourself.

I COULDN'T HELP OVERHEARING

IN PAIRS

The recording should be played twice. Students don't have to understand every word that's spoken, they just need to identify the topic of each phone call and who the speakers are talking to. On the second listening they should decide on a question they might ask the speakers to help them to understand the conversations more fully.
There are no 'correct answers' to this exercise, the notes below are just suggested answers. Allow everyone to put forward their own theories and explain how they reached their conclusions.

Who talking to	Topic	Question
1 Garage man	Car	What was the mistake?
2 A stranger	Meeting	Who was Marilyn really calling?
3 Shop assistant	Electric gadget	What kind of gadget is it?
4 Girlfriend or mistress	Meeting	Where are you meeting her?
5 Her assistant (?)	Visitors (policemen?)	What do the three visitors want?

Transcript

First speaker: . . . Hallo . . . hallo . . . no you called me. . . . Oh yes hallo . . . oh good . . . this afternoon, hmm, about what time? . . . What time do you close? . . . And about how much is it going to cost? . . . Pardon? . . . What? Are you sure? . . . Look, I think there's been some ghastly mistake. . . . Mine's a green Horizon. . . . Yes, green. . . . And the number's WBC 158X. . . . Yes, X. . . . No, no. If it's Y it must be someone else's. Could you just go and check? Thanks. . . . Hallo. . . . Right, good. . . . Mine was only in for a service. . . . Ha ha. . . . And when will it be ready? . . . Not till Monday? Oh goodness. . . . I need it at the weekend, we're going away to relations. . . . Can I speak to the manager, please? . . . Has he? Oh. . . . No, it's not your fault, sorry. . . . All right. . . . Could you . . . could you really? That's awfully kind of you. . . . About lunchtime? Fine. . . . Thanks very much indeed. . . . Bye.

Second speaker: . . . Hallo. Mary Smith speaking. . . . No John's not in at the moment. Can I take a message? . . . No, no, he's not in, I said. . . . Yes, he's at work. . . . Yes, really. . . . Er . . . would you like to leave a message? . . . All right. . . . Yes, yes, yes I have. . . . 'Marilyn will be expecting you this evening at 10.30'. Right, yes, I've got that. . . . That's all right, g . . . just . . . just a minute, did you say *this* evening? . . . I mean, I didn't know anything about this. . . . Yes, it *is* my business and no I'm not his sister! . . . I'm his wife, of course. . . . Who are you anyway? I've never heard of any Marilyn. . . . Ohhh! oh . . . are you sure you've got the right John Smith? . . . 574893. . . . Harrison Avenue. . . . No, not Harewood, Harrison. . . . Oh, you had me worried there for a few minutes. Oh no, don't worry, worry, it's an easy mistake to make . . . no no, really. . . . Fine. . . . Goodbye then. . . . Yes? . . . Ha ha yes . . . Bye.

Third speaker: . . . Yeah well I just can't get it to work. . . . Yeah, I've read them carefully. . . . Three times. . . . Well, the problem is I don't understand all the words. For example, what's the 'Lateral section pump . . . suction . . . suction pump switch'? . . . Is it? Well, why don't they say 'green switch' then. . . . I'm sorry but I am not an electrician and the book should be written so that anyone can understand what to do. . . . Yeah. . . . Which one? . . . On the top? Yeah, well it . . . it was pointing to the letter O. That stands for ON, doesn't it? . . . Really? . . . But then what does I stand for? . . . What do you mean 'one'? One what? . . . Zero? Good grief! You're joking. . . . So if I turn it to I or 'one' as you call it, then. . . . OK, I'll try that . . . but I still think there's a design fault somewhere. . . . If it doesn't go this time, I'll ring you back straight away. . . . Yeah, well thanks anyway. . . . Goodbye.

Fourth speaker: . . . I can't talk now, someone's just come in. . . . That's right, yes. I'm glad that's agreed then. . . . I'll ring you back when I've made some enquiries. . . . In about half an hour. . . . It's all right they've gone. . . . Yes, darling. . . . Yes, I miss you too . . . well, tomorrow's difficult, how about Tuesday? . . . Usual place? . . . Good. . . . I can hardly wait either. . . . Me too. . . . Of course I do. . . . I think there's someone coming in again. . . . Goodbye then. . . . And I'll look forward to seeing you then. . . . Absolutely. . . . Yes. . . . Goodbye, madam.

Fifth speaker: . . . No, no I can't. . . . We'll talk about it later. . . . No look, Peter, it's not the sort of thing I want to discuss over the phone. . . . Yes, I know there are three of them. . . . Well, I'm sorry but they'll just have to go on waiting until I get there. . . . As soon as I can. . . . No, look, the sooner I stop talking to you the sooner I can get in the car and come over there. . . . Only about ten minutes. . . . So just ask them to sit down and wait – offer them a cup of tea or something – and I'll be there as soon as I can. . . . All right then, that's better. See you in ten minutes then. Bye.

(Time 5 minutes 45 seconds)

SECRET MESSAGES

IN GROUPS OF 3 OR 4

A group that is stuck might need a few clues or a bit of guidance, but do allow a reasonable amount of time for them to try to sort it out for themselves first. Allow time also for replies to be encoded and sent to other groups.
The code works like this:

1	2	3	4	5	6	7	8	9	0
A	B	C	D	E	F	G	H	I	J
K	L	M	N	O	P	Q	R	S	T
U	V	W	X	Y	Z				

The full message reads:
'COME AT MIDNIGHT BRING A LADDER JULIET'
and a suitable reply might be:
95885   45   214458   551   3922   8125   05   0136!

SHORT AND SWEET

IN PAIRS

This activity is inspired by an exchange of messages between Victor Hugo and his publisher:
Victor Hugo's message was '?' and the publisher replied '!'. See if the class can work out what they meant.
If there is time, get your students to expand each of the exchanges into telephone conversations (back to back again) and then compose their own brief exchanges for another pair to interpret.

WRITTEN WORK

1 Write four short letters giving the same information as *one* of the
   telegram exchanges shown in 'Short and sweet' on page 17.
2 Write a letter re-establishing contact with an old friend you haven't
   been in touch with for a year.
3 Write three postcards to a friend abroad:
   one from where you are now
   one from a favourite holiday resort
   one from a place you don't like

5 In and out of town

This unit deals with comparing life in cities and in the country, and with talking about visits to cities and to the countryside.

Vocabulary

towns and cities
capital, village, suburb, slums, shanty town, district, city centre (downtown), county, state, region, province

places in towns
cinema (theater), theatre, opera house, concert hall, leisure centre, railway station (railroad station), bus station, police station, underground/tube (subway/metro)
streets, square, park, gardens, avenue, (block)

countryside
view, scenery, beauty spot, horizon, viewpoint
hill, mountain, slope, cliff, valley, plain, desert, marsh, forest, wood, jungle, clearing, volcano
river, stream, waterfall, canal, lake
footpath, lane, hedge, fence, ditch

buildings and farms
castle, palace, manor house, farm house, cottage, barn
field, orchard, vineyard, meadow, crops, harvest, hay
TO.... grow, harvest, pick, sow, plant, plough (plow)

country people
farmer, peasant, farm worker, landowner, shepherd, countryman/woman, gamekeeper

fauna – students should know the names of the common animals to be found in their country. In Britain these might be:
domestic animals: cow, sheep, goat, donkey, chicken, goose, duck, turkey, pig
wild animals, birds and insects: fox, squirrel, rabbit, hare, deer, seagull, pigeon, sparrow, owl, snake, frog, ant, mosquito, wasp, bee

flora – similarly:
trees: oak, beech, pine, fir, palm
flowers: daisy, buttercup, dandelion

THERE'S NO PLACE LIKE HOME

IN PAIRS

The pre-listening discussion could be done in pairs, as suggested, or the whole class could be involved. Make sure everyone does make notes on the chart before the recording is played.

Here are the points the speakers in the radio programme made – your students' versions will look different because of their own notes and the ticks they make:

Advantages of living in a village		Advantages of living in a large city	
Friendly people Fresh air Healthy life Safe Less crime than city Less traffic Cheaper accommodation Quiet and peaceful		More entertainment Open-minded people Stores and shops Opportunity to make new friends	

Transcript

Chairman: We're here tonight in the lovely Suffolk village of Tuddenham, where we're the guests of the Tuddenham Women's Institute. Our team tonight is Henry Mitchell the Canadian broadcaster and writer, Mary Johnson the actress and Jenny Martin the journalist. And our first question comes from. . . .

Villager: Janet Parker. If the members of the team could choose where to live, would they live in a village or in a city?

Chairman: Thank you, Mrs Parker.

Villager: Miss!

Chairman: Sorry . . . er . . . Miss Parker. If the members of the team could choose where to live, would they live in a village or in a city? Henry.

Henry: Well, I think I'd prefer to live in a village because . . . well, I think the people are friendly and there's a lot of fresh air. I think life generally is healthier in a village and I like being close to nature. And it's very easy for my work as a writer to have peace and quiet.

Chairman: Mary.

Mary: Well, I'd prefer to live in a city because there's more going on. Er . . . being an actress, I need to go to the cinema and the theatre and there's far more entertainment in the city than there is in the country, of course. I also like it because . . . um . . . people are more open-minded. People don't . . . um . . . mind what you do in the city. And for the shopping as well, I mean, I love going to the village shop but the stores and shops in London can't compare with anything.

Chairman: You don't think the . . . er . . . the city can be lonely?

Mary: Oh, no, no. You can . . . have to go out and make friends. And. . . .

Chairman: Good, fine.

Mary: . . . .at least there's the opportunity in London.

Chairman: Jenny.

Jenny: Yes, well, I prefer living in a village. It's safer than a city and there's less crime and of course there's less traffic, so it's much more pleasant. Then, it's much cheaper than the city. There are . . . you know, rents are cheaper and so of course are house prices. It's quiet, it's . . . it's peaceful. Yes, I much prefer living in a village.

Chairman: Jolly good, all right. Well, thank you very much indeed. And let's find out where the members of the team really do live. Henry?

Henry: Well, I live in London because I have to do a lot of travelling and it's more convenient, but I don't like living there.

Chairman: Fine. Er . . . Mary?

Mary: Oh, I live in a village rather like this one – because my husband is a farmer.

Chairman: I see, but you'd . . . er . . . you don't really like that situation?

Mary: I'm afraid I don't!

Chairman: Oh dear, oh dear. Jenny?

Jenny: Yes, well I have the best of both worlds, I'm afraid. I live in a small town which is within easy reach of London and it's very close to the country.

Chairman: Mmm, very nice too. OK, well, thank you very much. And our next question is from. . . .

(Time: 2 minutes 45 seconds)

WHERE IS . . . ? 🎴

IN PAIRS

Student A looks at activity 11, while student B looks at activity 39. Each
is given different information about the city of Bath: A knows about
shops, car parks and public transport; B knows about the sights and
places of interest. Each has the same basic map, so they can explain to
each other where everything is.

A DAY OUT

IN PAIRS OR GROUPS OF 3 OR 4

Further discussion can be provoked by asking each group to cut down
their list to just 3 items. Allow time for the groups to meet with each
other and to explain their choices – or cross-groups could be formed,
composed of members of different groups.

A DAY IN LONDON 🎴

IN PAIRS

Make sure you have an *even number* of pairs and if necessary have
among them two groups of 3 to make up even numbers. Half of the
pairs should look at activity 5, while the other half look at activity 28.
Each pair is given information about a different part of London (the
City or Westminster) and has to plan a half-day's visit there. When the
plans are complete, the pairs join up with each other to form groups of 4
and the different plans are explained and discussed. Make sure each
group of 4 is composed of pairs from the different 'sides'.

A DAY IN THE COUNTRY

IN GROUPS OF 3 OR 4

If the members of the class are unfamiliar with the area they are
studying in, it might be a good idea to start the ball rolling by having a
general discussion about the area and making a list of attractions and
beauty spots on the board. Each group can then select places from this
list for their tour and decide on the route they will take. A map of the
area should be on show if possible.

I NEED A BREAK. . . .

IN GROUPS OF 3 OR 4

After each group has noted down its ideas, form pairs of students from different groups.
Here is the complete text of the advertisement, for your information – the language may be too idiomatic for your students.

URBAN MAN.
Note the pasty complexion and haggard, haunted expression. The glazed, sunken eyes, looking out for the next executive crisis.
This man needs help. He needs a complete change of environment. A restful weekend in the English countryside.
Fortunately for him the new *Let's Go* guide is just out. It lists country hotels in England offering special weekend rates from now until spring.
By referring to the guide he'll be able to select a suitable country retreat, where he should do nothing more arduous than observe the leaves fall

to the ground and the clouds pass across the sky. The only question to tax his mind should be why sycamore leaves fall with a heavy resounding thud, beech leaves flutter down aimlessly and chestnut leaves spin like tops.
Not that he'll be totally free from high-

"I need to slow down for a few days..."

powered /decision making. He'll have to decide whether/to amble left, up a winding country lane, or right, down a winding country lane. Whether to gather catkins or sticky-buds. Whether it's the chaffinch that has a yellow breast, or the bullfinch.
Nor will he be able to turn his back on matters of high-finance. How many coins should he drop into the box for the repair of the fifteenth century village church? Will his funds run to a second glass of locally-brewed real ale from the wood?
Following this spot of rest and recuperation, Urban Man will rapidly see the effects of his change of pace.
The colour will return to his cheeks. The furrow will disappear from his brow. And his expression of anguish will turn into an expression of calm contentment.

English Tourist Board

Let's Go 1981/2 lists over 1100 hotels throughout England offering reduced weekend rates during the off-season. Send this coupon for a free copy.

Name

Address

LG R12

To: English Tourist Board,
Let's Go,
Hendon Road,
Sunderland
SR9 9XZ.

RURAL MAN.
Note the weather-beaten complexion and doleful expression. The impassive eyes, suggesting (not to put too fine a point on it) that he is out of touch.

This man needs help. He needs a complete change of environment.

A reckless weekend in an English city.

Fortunately for him the new *Let's Go* guide is just out. It lists city hotels in England offering special weekend rates from now until spring.

By looking up the guide he'll be able to select a base for his attack on the city, where he'll quickly broaden his horizons.

On a theatre trip for instance, he may be provoked, enlightened, thrilled or amused, but in any event, he'll see leading actors and actresses tread the boards in the flesh, rather than through a cathode-ray tube.

Touring the city shops he'll see all the latest fashions on display, not just hanging from rails, but actually being worn by the customers.

At the art galleries, he'll have an opportunity to hob-nob with old-masters and post-impressionists and later, when he feels peckish, he'll discover works of the culinary art his taste buds never knew existed.

Then after dark he'll be tempted by another choice of diversions. Cabaret at a sophisticated nightspot. A merry tour of the city's watering-holes. Or perhaps even the unthinkable, a quick sortie onto the floor of a discotheque.

Following this wild city experience, Rural Man will rapidly see the effects of his change of pace. The sparkle will return to his eyes.

The old alert expression will reassert itself. And his previously blinkered outlook will turn into one of acute awareness.

"I need some fast-living for a few days..."

English Tourist Board

Let's Go 1981/2 lists over 1100 hotels throughout England offering reduced weekend rates during the off-season. Send this coupon for a free copy.

Name_____

Address_____

LG&T3

To: English Tourist Board, Let's Go, Hendon Road, Sunderland SR9 9XZ.

WRITTEN WORK

1 What do you enjoy about living in your own city, town or village? Write about the pleasures and advantages of living there.

2 Imagine someone is coming to stay with you and has to find his or her way to your home from the railway (or bus) station. Write a letter explaining how to get there.

3 Write a description of the countryside around the place you live. Try to imagine how it would strike a foreigner: what's unusual, interesting or pleasant about the area?

6 Stranger than fiction

This unit deals with talking about the unexplained and about amazing events and coincidences.

Vocabulary

phenomena
event, phenomenon, happening, coincidence, mystery, puzzle, miracle fate, chance, bad luck, fortune, jinx, accident, supernatural, magic, déjà vu

reactions
strange, weird, odd, peculiar, funny, curious, amazing, extraordinary, unbelievable, remarkable, surprising, astounding

people
fortune teller, forecaster, clairvoyant, medium, sceptic, believer, ghost, poltergeist, little green man, visitor from another planet

luck
Keep your fingers crossed, touch wood, good luck, all the best, that's life (that's how the cookie crumbles), you never know

star signs
Aquarius, Pisces, Aries, Taurus, Gemini, Cancer, Leo, Virgo, Libra, Scorpio, Sagittarius, Capricorn (note the English pronunciation of each)

1900 📼

The facts given are absolutely true. Here is a model answer to the exercise.

1 They looked identical.

2 Both had wives called Marie.

3 Both had sons called Vittorio.

4 They were born on the same day.

5 They were born at exactly the same time of day.

6 Both 'went into business' in the same year.

7 Both taking part in sports contest.

8 Both shot.

(9? Both died instantly.)

Transcript

John: . . .there he was standing right there in the street exac. . . on the day when I'd thought about it, yeah.

Sue: No, that's incredible, what a coincidence! But listen, have you ever heard the story of King Umberto I of Italy?

John: No.

Sue: Well, this is absolutely true, that on – I think it was July 28 in
1 1900 – King Umberto I was introduced to a man who owned a restaurant in Milan and they were absolutely identical, they looked just like each other. They got talking and found out that
2 this man's wife was called Marie and so was the King's. And
3 they both had sons called Vittorio.

John: Was that the coincidence?

Sue: Well, that's just one of them, that's two of them, wait for it. They had both . . . both these men . . . both the King and the
4 restaurant owner had been born on the same day at exactly the
5 same time . . . and they'd both gone . . . well, the restaurant owner had gone into business . . . er . . . quite late on in life and
6 the same year King Umberto became king, OK? Now, one day . . . um . . . the King was going to give the prizes at a sports contest near Milan and the other guy was going to take part in
7 the same contest in the shooting contest. Anyway, that evening the restaurant owner accidentally shot himself when he was cleaning his gun and . . . and died instantly. Anyway, next day the King was on his way to the contest when he heard the news of this man's death and he was just about to go and pay
8 his last respects and see the body when *he* was shot – on

purpose by an Italian-born anarchist from New Jersey, who was a silk weaver I think, who'd come back to his native land especially to assassinate the King. And the King died instantly, too.

John: Now, is that true?

Sue: Absolutely true.

(Time: 1 minute 45 seconds)

100 YEARS

IN PAIRS

The pictures show Abraham Lincoln (half close your eyes to see him) and John F. Kennedy (out of focus).
Student A has more information about Kennedy in activity 7.
Student B has more information about Lincoln in activity 47.
There are a number of (uncanny?) coincidences contained in the texts and the pairs should try to discover these and later comment on them.

By the way, numerous astrologers warned Kennedy that he would be killed on that day in Dallas, but he insisted on being driven through the streets with the car's bullet-proof plastic bubble top removed, and refused to change any of his plans. Did the astrologers know what was going to happen, do you think, really?

IDENTICAL TWINS?

EVERYONE

After they have read the text (which is perfectly genuine) everyone should stand up and try to find how many of the class share the same ages, birth signs, family backgrounds and interests. Tell them they are looking for their 'twin'.

If there is much interest in astrology, it might be worth going through the names of the star signs in English with the class, and practising their pronunciation.

TRUE OR FALSE?

IN PAIRS OR GROUPS OF 3

1   True, approximately.
2   True, there was a tidal wave.
3   True, but only very young babies can.
4   False, a cold is a virus you catch from other people.
5   False, another is the Mexican peso.
6   False, the odds remain 1 in 2 (evens) however many tosses have been made before.
7   False, though they may sometimes appear to be more mature.
8   False, you might only *believe* this if you went from west to east.

9   True: Europe (excluding USSR) 482 million, USA 227 million.
10   True, try it!
11   False, everyone does but some people don't remember them.
12   False, space exploration has proved this now. Perhaps in another solar system, though.
13   True.
14   False, the line would be 55 km long.
15   True.
16   True.
17   True: sweet, sour, salt, bitter.
18   False, a whale isn't a fish but a mammal.

In case any group need a clue, you could reveal that *half* the statements are false.

THE CAMERA CANNOT LIE

IN PAIRS

Accept the best stories offered – no correct solutions are given here because everyone should be encouraged to be as imaginative as possible. The most fanciful story is likely to be the best and most amusing.

ARE YOU SUPERSTITIOUS?

IN PAIRS

Different cultures have different superstitions. Try to mix the nationalities in a multinational class. Tell the class your own answers to the questionnaire (perhaps inventing some less rational superstitions?) and invite comments.

IT'S ALL IN THE MIND

IN GROUPS OF 4

There could be meat here for several quite passionate discussions. Allow each group to choose which topics to deal with in depth and which to leave till later if they have time.

WRITTEN WORK

1   Write your own opinions about one of the phenomena mentioned in 'It's all in the mind' on page 25.
2   Write a story inspired by one of the photos in 'The camera cannot lie' on page 24.
3   Describe a coincidence or set of coincidences that have happened to you or to someone you know.

7 Going places

This unit deals with talking about travelling by public transport and by car, and giving directions to people.

Vocabulary

transport
airliner, jet, plane, helicopter, hovercraft, airship, hydrofoil, tram, bus, trolleybus, coach (bus), underground (subway), train, liner, ferry, steamer, cruise ship

people
pilot/captain, crew, cabin staff, ground staff/ground crew, steward, stewardess (flight attendant)
captain/master, seaman/sailor, crew, officer
driver, conductor, guard, inspector

flying
runway, departure lounge, control tower, terminal
take off, landing, flight, connection

railways (railroads)
station (depot), left-luggage office (baggage room), ticket office, platform
engine, carriage (car), buffet car, restaurant car
ticket, single (one-way), return (round trip), reservation

travelling
To ... travel, commute, fly, sail, arrive at, depart from, leave for, go by

vehicles
car, saloon (sedan), estate (station wagon), hatchback, lorry (truck), van, caravan (trailer), dormobile (camper), motorcycle/motorbike, scooter, moped

parts of a car
windscreen (windshield), boot (trunk), headlights, indicators, clutch, brakes, accelerator (gas pedal), gear lever (gear shift), seat belt, engine, carburettor (carburetor), radiator

people
motorist, driver, passenger, cyclist, motorcyclist, pedestrian, traffic policeman, traffic warden, mechanic

places
garage, petrol station (gas station), car park (parking lot), drive (driveway), parking space, parking meter, traffic lights, pedestrian crossing, subway (pedestrian underpass)

roads
street, lane, avenue, motorway (freeway), dual carriageway (divided highway), bypass, pavement (sidewalk), footpath, main road, side road, one-way street, no entry, junction (intersection), crossroads, corner, bend, roundabout (traffic circle), tunnel, bridge

driving
TO... drive, steer, ride, change gear, pull up/stop, pull in/stop at the kerb, pull out/drive off into the traffic, brake, accelerate, part, have an accident, crash, skid

direction
TO... turn left/right, bear left/right/fork left/right, go straight on, follow the signs for, you can't miss it!

IT'S THE ONLY WAY TO TRAVEL 🔲 🔳

IN 3 GROUPS

Divide the class into 3 groups: group A should look at communication activity 1, group B at activity 21 and group C at activity 42. Each group is given a different attitude to the conversation they are about to hear. After they have heard it, the 3 groups should be recombined into groups of 3, each consisting of members of different groups.
(Group A are all afraid of flying, group B are all coach-sick and group C are all against train travel.)

Times	Advantages	Disadvantages
PLANE left London at *9.15* arrived in Plymouth at *10.30*	Quick Beautiful view	Have to get to Gatwick Airport Only 3 planes a day Expensive
TRAIN left London at *10.30* arrived in Plymouth at *1.30*	Frequent service (hourly) Modern, comfortable trains Lovely view from dining car	Quite crowded Quite expensive
COACH left London at *8.20* arrived in Plymouth at *14.00*	Cheap Comfortable Air-conditioned coaches 5 coaches a day + one overnight	5½ hour journey

Transcript

Douglas: Ah! that's much better!

Charles: Ah! That's yours, I think . . . er . . . Doug.

Douglas: Thank you very much, Charles.

Charles: Right. You have a good journey then, Douglas?

Douglas: Yes I did, I did. I must say the plane was marvellous, marvellous.

Charles: Very quick, then?

Douglas: Er . . . the plane journey was terrifically quick . . . er . . . I mean, you . . . er . . . what . . . you met me about 9 . . . er . . . what . . . er . . . 10 . . . 10.45.

Charles: About half past ten.

Douglas: Yes, the plane got in at . . . er . . . 10.30 and we left Gatwick at 9.15.

Charles: What time did you have to start though in the morning?

Douglas: Well, that was . . . er . . . that was a different story, because I had to get to Victoria . . . um . . . at . . . you know, to get to Gatwick and it's . . . er . . . from . . . er . . . Victoria to Gatwick's three quarters of an hour. Then I had to leave home at 7.30 and get up at 6.30.

Charles: Oh, gracious me!

Douglas: So I'm not sure if you save much really.

Charles: Jet travel, my goodness me! It was worth the experience, though?

Douglas: Oh, I mean, you know, I've never flown across the South of England and it really looked absolutely fantastic, especially as we proach . . . approached Plymouth, you know, with this sunshine and it looked really marvellous . . . marvellous.

Charles: Well, when you come up next time, would you be coming the same way?

Douglas: Oh, I don't think so. I don't . . . to be honest. . . .

Charles: Well, why not?

Douglas: Well, to be honest it was a bit of a luxury because it was a really expensive flight and of course there are only 3 planes a day. Well, luckily you could meet me at . . . er . . . 10.30. . . . Hallo, isn't that . . . um . . . Annabel!

Charles: Oh it is, it's Annabel.
Douglas: Over here, over here!
Annabel: Hallo!
Charles: Nice to see you, my dear.
Annabel: Hallo there, how are you?
Charles: Want a drink, my dear?
Annabel: Yes, please.
Charles: Right, I'll . . . er . . . fix them. You had a good journey?
Annabel: Yes, I had a lovely time, I came by train . . . er . . . it was . . . er. . . .
Charles: What time did you start then?
Annabel: Oh, about half past ten I think. Got here about half past one. So it's
           only . . . what . . . three hours. Very quick.
Charles: Very good. Douglas came up by plane!
Annabel: Oh, how fancy! Well, this was . . . er . . . this was a nice train, you
           know, very modern and comfortable. And of course loads of trains –
           about every hour I think.
Charles: Oh, great. Did you get something to eat on the train?
Annabel: Yes thanks, yes. Had a nice lunch. Oh, it's wonderful, you can sit
           there drinking your soup and watching the view go by. I like it. . . .
Douglas: I bet it's a . . . it's a hell of a lot cheaper than the plane.
Annabel: Well, actually, I thought it was quite expensive . . . um . . . unless
           you've got, you know, a student card or something.
Douglas: Oh, those days are long gone!
Annabel: But it was quite . . . quite crowded. I was . . . I was glad I'd booked a
           seat, you know.
Douglas: Yes, yes.
Charles: Yes. And if it . . . it . . . it's Belinda! Hallo!
Belinda: Hallo.
Annabel: Hallo, Belinda.
Douglas: Hallo.
Charles: Right on time, my dear.
Belinda: Well, I've had a most wonderful journey.
Charles: Really?
Belinda: On the coach. Yes!
Charles: Good Lord!
Belinda: And it was really cheap. I thought I'd try it because I haven't got very
           many pennies at the moment.
Charles: You didn't have to start last night, did you?
Belinda: No, no, no! I set off at about . . . um . . . twenty past eight and I got
           here at round about two o'clock.
Charles: Good!
Belinda: And it was really good and it was really comfortable as well.
Charles: A lot of motorway travel, then?
Belinda: Well, there was a lot of motorway travel. Because there was a lot of
           motorway travel I was able to read . . . to sit and read my book. And
           it was a really smooth journey. . . .
Annabel: Didn't you get travel sick?
Belinda: No, I didn't feel sick at all.

Douglas: They're really hot, those coaches!

Belinda: Well, it was air-conditioned, actually, and it was really nice.

Charles: Well, you must have been nearly six hours in the coach. Wasn't that very tiring?

Belinda: Yes, I suppose about five and a half hours, but I mean once I started looking at my book, you know I didn't notice the time at all. It just flew by. It's incredible.

Charles: What's the service like, then? I mean, are there a lot of coaches?

Belinda: I think it's pretty good ... er ... there are about five coaches in the day and there's one overnight coach as well, I believe. So it's really nice.

Charles: Splendid. Well. . . .

Douglas: Anyone for another drink?

Charles: Oh, I don't know.

Belinda: Haven't had my first yet. . . .

(Time: 3 minutes 20 seconds)

TRANSPORT SURVEY

IN 4 GROUPS AT FIRST

A very large class might have 6 groups to start with. Each group designs its own questionnaire, possibly with a little help from you, and then members of the group go out and interview members of other groups. In this way each student can engage in three separate one-to-one interviews. Make sure people keep moving round during the interview phase – of course, everyone will have to stand up.

ON THE ROAD

IN PAIRS OR GROUPS OF 3

The photo and the questions are just 'starters'. Hopefully the discussion will lead to an exchange of information and opinions about traffic generally. Make sure each group devotes time to the 'advice to a foreign visitor' activity; later the groups can exchange ideas on this topic.

LET'S GO! [✦]

IN PAIRS

Student A looks at activity 16, while Student B looks at 29. A role-played telephone conversation ensues (back to back again) about travel arrangements for a trip to and from New York from Britain. Student A has to travel from Bristol and Student B from London. Each is provided with timetables giving different (but complementary) information.

THOSE WERE THE DAYS

IN GROUPS OF 3

Nostalgia time – or rather, imagination time. You may need to hurry some groups up to deal with each of the four parts of this activity.

EXCUSE ME...

IN PAIRS

This activity will need to be modified if students are talking about a smallish town or even a smallish city. If they know their own capital city they should talk about that unless their own city has a fairly complex public transport system. Instead of arriving at the airport, the guests could arrive at the railway station, or even the bus station.

FOUR TRANSPORT PUZZLES

IN PAIRS OR GROUPS OF 3

The solutions are:
1 Neither (They will be the same distance from London.)
2 10km ($90 + 30 = 120$km/h closing speed; 5 minutes is $\frac{1}{12}$ hour.)
3 3 hours (He fell asleep after $4\frac{1}{2}$ hours, and woke up $1\frac{1}{2}$ hours before reaching his destination.)
4 About 12 (because he will be passed by trains that left Cockfosters during the *previous* hour as well as during the hour he was travelling. Nasty!)

WRITTEN WORK

1 What kinds of transport do you like most and dislike most? Write two paragraphs explaining why.
2 Describe a journey you'll always remember.
3 Look at 'Those were the days' on page 28 and write your thoughts on one (or two) of the questions there.

8 A quiet evening in

This unit deals with talking about television and radio programmes, and describing hobbies and other leisure activities.

Vocabulary

television
TV, telly/the box (the tube), show, programme (program), broadcast, film (movie), serial, series, play, chat show (talk show), soap opera, documentary, commercial/advertisement

radio
short wave, long wave, medium wave (AM), VHF (FM)

music
pop, rock, classical, chamber, choral, operatic, jazz, folk, dance orchestra, band, group, quartet

musicians
guitarist, violinist, drummer, bass player, pianist, composer, conductor

instruments and equipment
banjo, organ, saxophone, French horn, clarinet, flute, violin, cello, baton, record player, hi-fi, cassette player, radio, music centre, single, LP (album), cassette

leisure and hobbies see also Unit 20 'It's only a game'
leisure, free time, spare time, recreation, hobby, pastime, interest, activity
reading, photography, stamp-collecting, model-building, playing cards: bridge, poker, etc., keeping pets: mice, guinea pigs, gerbils, etc.
entertaining, amusing, fascinating, interesting, absorbing
(Make sure everyone knows the English words for their own hobbies and perhaps their friends' or family's hobbies, too.)

cooking see also Unit 10 'A night out'
ingredients
meat: beef, pork, lamb, veal, ham, bacon, chicken, steak, joint (roast), chop, cutlet, liver, kidneys

vegetables: cauliflower, asparagus, cabbage, carrots, onions, celery,
  tomatoes, mushrooms
fish: trout, shrimps, prawns (shrimps), crab, sole, tuna, sardine
fats: oil, butter, lard, margarine
herbs: parsley, basil, tarragon, oregano, sage, thyme, rosemary
spices: cinnamon, nutmeg, ginger
seasoning: salt and pepper
fruit: banana, grape, peach, pear, apricot, grapefruit, pineapple
bread, roll, cake, tart, pie, pancake, biscuits (cookies), scones (biscuits)
sauce, gravy, stock, juice, soup

cooking
TO... mix, stir, beat, whip, cut, slice, carve, chop, mince, peel, grate,
  spread, cook, roast, grill (broil), fry, stew, bake, steam

cooking utensils and equipment
saucepan, frying pan (skillet), mixer, liquidiser, food processor,
  chopping board, bowl, dish, washing-up bowl, dishwasher

Warning! Don't get too technical unless the majority of a class are really
into cooking and want to know precise expressions to talk about this
interest of theirs!

WHAT'S ON THE BOX?

IN PAIRS

The recorded extract from a radio programme is intended to provide
extra information and not necessarily confound the students' plans.

Transcript

Sue: ...and if we hear any further news we'll let you know right away.
          Well, now it's time for our regular look at this evening's viewing and
          here's Patrick Lloyd, television critic of the *Daily Mail*. Hallo, Patrick.
Patrick: Hallo, Sue.
Sue: Patrick, what's worth watching this evening?
Patrick: Well, Sue, it's a very good night on all four channels and I think my
          first recommendation would be the documentary on ITV at 8.30. It's
          an amazing film about the history and growth of the British Secret
          Service, MI5. Now it's the first time many of the facts have been made
          public and it's about the growth of what was originally called Military
          Intelligence Department 5 into the UK equivalent of the CIA or KGB.

Sue: Mmm, sounds well worth . . . watching.

Patrick: Now, after that and still on ITV at 9.30 there's another documentary.
          In 'World in Action' there's an investigation of multinational
          industries and this one concentrates on the food and drink industries. I
          wonder, Sue, did you know for example that Heinz Foods are the
          owners of Weightwatchers International?

Sue: No, really?

Patrick: Over on Channel 4 at 7: 'Watch Your Step'. Two teams of university
          teachers and students have to survive for 24 hours in the North of
          Scotland and they've got to solve various problems to reach their goal.
          They don't get any help and they have to do things like find clues,
          solve puzzles, work out how to cross rivers, how to climb cliffs, make
          a fire, cook food. Sounds a bit daft but it really is an exciting
          programme that makes you, the viewer, think too. Well worth seeing.

Sue: Ha ha, rather them than me! Now, anything for sports fans?

Patrick: Yes, football on BBC 1 at 7.50 – that's live coverage of England v
          Brazil and tennis on BBC 2 at 10 with the best of today's play from
          Wimbledon.

Sue: And what about films?

Patrick: Ah, lots of good films on tonight, Sue. My pick of the bunch would be
          'High Plains Drifter' starring Clint Eastwood. It's not just another one
          of those violent westerns and . . . um . . . in fact it's a really remarkable
          film. A kind of allegory of the battle between good and evil. The
          photography is superb and although the film wasn't really appreciated
          when it was first released in 1972, it's well worth seeing on the small
          screen. And this is on ITV at 10.30.

Sue: All right. Thanks very much, Patrick.

Patrick: Now, hold on, just one more thing I ought to mention and that's the
          television production of Shakespeare's *Hamlet* on Channel 4 at 9. It's
          got a cast of little-known actors and it's got sub-titles.

Sue: Sub-titles?

Patrick: Yes, that's right. Channel 4 have taken the bold step of putting sub-
          titles on the screen in modern English. It may sound strange, even . . .
          even perhaps distracting, but believe me, it works remarkably well.
          After all, the English language has changed quite a bit in the last 400
          years.

Sue: All right, thanks very much, Patrick.

Patrick: Not at all.

Sue: That sounds as though it's worth staying in for tonight. And now let's
          hear from Ian Duncan at the sports desk. . . .

(Time: 2 minutes 35 seconds)

DID YOU SEE. . .?

IN PAIRS

No 'correct' version of the story is given here – students should use their imaginations and experience of similar programmes.

WHAT HAPPENED AT THE END?

IN PAIRS OR GROUPS OF 3

Here are some possible endings to each extract. They are not definitive and your students' guesses may be as good as mine!

'. . .committed the murder is Mr Robertson himself.' (Murder at the Vicarage)
'. . .honey.' (The Private Life of the Bee)
'. . .rain.' (Weather – BBC 2, 7 o'clock)
'. . .coal.' (?) '. . .grass.' (?) (Science Now)
'. . .Coca Cola.' (World in Action)
'. . .I'm expecting a baby.' (Love Story)

Again, it isn't necessary for every word to be understood to be able to guess the answers. Ask students to explain the reasons for their conclusions.

Transcript

Robertson: (the butler)	But there's no other way it could have been done, madam. I clearly saw Mr Mendel crossing the lawn with it in his hand.
Mrs Wallace:	Robertson, you know that's only supposition. Now, what possible proof have you got? After all, Mr Mendel is in a wheelchair. Now how can he. . . ?
Inspector Drew:	I'm sorry to interrupt, Mrs Wallace, but I think we have been overlooking one very important point. Something we should have realised some time ago.
Mrs Wallace:	Really, Inspector?
Inspector Drew:	Yes, I mean that at 6 o'clock in the morning at this time of year it's not yet light. And on the night in question, there was no moon. In other words Mr Robertson couldn't possibly have seen Mr Mendel – or anyone else for that matter.
Mrs Wallace:	You mean. . . ?
Inspector Drew:	Yes, I mean that the only person in this house who could have. . . .

Man: . . .it's an entirely natural product. To produce one pound it has been calculated that one worker would need to fly a total distance equivalent to four orbits of the earth. Of course that's impossible because they only live for 6 weeks on average and only half their life is spent actually collecting pollen and nectar. So in fact it's a co-operative effort really between the 50,000 workers in each hive and yield from one hive can vary between 5 and 10 pounds of . . .

Woman: . . . and an anticyclone near the Azores. So we seem to be stuck between the two, which means that it will continue to be unsettled for a while. Towards evening there may be fog patches in all areas. Looking now at tomorrow's chart, as you can see there's a likelihood of further . . .

Reporter: . . . here in Ireland, a country with few natural resources, the problem of fuel imports has always been a great one. But now what could prove to be a breakthrough has been made at the University of Galway. We've reported in the programme in the past about cars driven by alcohol made from sugar cane in Brazil, driven by natural gas in Holland and by electricity in the USA but recent experiments have shown that a petrol substitute can be made cheaply from another material. This car I'm driving at the moment looks like any other car but believe it or not this car is powered by . . .

Voice: . . . Professor James Randolph of the London School of Economics.

Professor Randolph: In terms of political and economic power the biggest of them have a lot more influence than any third world nation and indeed more than many Western nations. I'm not just referring to oil companies or motor manufacturers here but take, for example, a company in the food and drink industry. One of these is the world's largest consumer of granulated sugar, has the world's second largest fleet of trucks and the world's largest retail sales force and is in fact the world's most advertised product. I'm talking of course about . . .

Sharon: But, Mum, don't you see that I . . .

Mum: Now listen to me, dear, you have your future to consider. If you stay at school and pass your exams, you'll be able to go to college and make a success of your life.

Sharon: But Mum . . .

Mum: Don't keep saying 'But Mum', my girl. If your father was still with us, he'd say just the same that I'm saying. You've got the brains, though you certainly didn't get them from me or your poor dad, and if you work hard you can do well. We never had the chances you've got. Anyway, you're far too young to get married.

Sharon: But, Mum, we've got to get married because . . .

(Time: 3 minutes 30 seconds)

MY TOP TEN

IN GROUPS OF 3 OR 4

Mixed nationality groups might be best in a multinational class. While students are filling in their choices, do the same yourself – they will probably be curious to know what your favourites are!

IT'S VERY GOOD BUT...

IN GROUPS OF 3 OR 4

In this activity students have a chance to be as polite and tactful, sarcastic or brutal as they wish!

BUSY DOING NOTHING?

IN PAIRS

The photos show:
sewing
lithography
stamp-collecting
medal-collecting
photography

COME ROUND TO MY PLACE!

IN GROUPS OF 4 OR 5

A class who are very interested in food could spend quite a long time on this activity. A less interested class should not be allowed to get bogged down in technical vocabulary.

WRITTEN WORK

1 Write a summary of the story of a film you've seen recently or a book you've read.
2 What's your hobby? Describe it enthusiastically so that someone who hasn't tried it might become interested.
3 Write a critical review of a TV programme, book or record you've recently seen, read or listened to. Imagine you're writing for the arts page of a newspaper.

9 Once upon a time

This unit deals with talking about past events and experiences.

Vocabulary

Time
*once, once upon a time, a long time ago, at one time, ages ago, some
time ago, donkey's years ago, when I was little, the day before
yesterday, a fortnight ago (two weeks ago)*
in the end, finally, last of all, at last
from 1979 to 1981, from May to July
*since 1981, since June, since the middle of last month, since last night,
since 8 o'clock*
for a few years, for months, for weeks, for 3 days

During this unit watch out for *irregular past verb forms* – if there are a
lot of errors, do some remedial work, perhaps using *Use of English* (CUP
1984). Also watch out for the correct use of:
past, present perfect simple, present perfect continuous and past perfect.
But don't worry too much about mistakes unless exams are in the offing:
for many learners a sentence like 'I've written it the day before
yesterday' is a fairly unimportant mistake, since it doesn't affect
communication at all.

I REMEMBER . . .

IN PAIRS

Here are model answers to the task set in this exercise.

What do you remember about:	Jack	Shirley
Your first holiday?	Homesick at aunt's house at the seaside	Lake District: honey and porridge for breakfast
Your first day at school?	Wanted to take his toys- took Teddy	Very frightened and shy
Your favourite teacher?	Miss Robson - kind, marvellous storyteller	Miss Brown - made history come to life

>>>→

	Jack	Shirley
What do you remember about:		
Your worst teacher?	Mr Goodman- pulled his ear	Mrs Sharpe-impatient maths teacher
Your last day at school?	Bucket of water fell on Mr Goodman	She cried

Transcript

Presenter: In this edition of our series 'Children of a Decade' I'll be talking to Jack Thompson, who was born in 1940, and to Shirley Sutton, who was born in 1930. First of all, Jack, thanks for joining us. Perhaps...

Jack: Not at all.

Presenter: Perhaps you'd tell us about your memories of your first holiday away from home?

Jack: Oh... yes... um... at age ten I think it was, yes, I went to stay with an aunt at the seaside. Well, it wasn't a very happy experience. I felt very homesick at first.

Presenter: Mmm. And what about your first day at school, can you remember that?

Jack: Yes, I can. Er... er... I was five years old and I wanted to take all my toys with me but... er... they wouldn't let me. In the end it was agreed that I could take my teddy... er... but only on the first day.

Presenter: Oh, I see. Your school days, were they happy ones?

Jack: Well... er... I didn't have a very good time at school – I wasn't very bright, you see. And the teachers didn't seem to like me, but... er... I made a lot of friends and some of them I still keep in touch with. One of them I married.

Presenter: Oh, that's wonderful. Well, did you have a favourite teacher?

Jack: Miss Robinson... or was it... no, it was Miss Robson. My first teacher, that's right yeah... very kind. Marvellous storyteller.

Presenter: And who was your worst teacher?

Jack: Mr Goodman, that's right. We used to call him 'Goody'. Yeah, he pulled your ear if you made a mistake or talked in class. Yeah, my left ear is still bigger, look.

Presenter: Ha ha. Perhaps you can tell us about your last day at school?

Jack: My last day, oh yeah, that's emblazoned on my mind. Oh, I wanted to get my own back you see on old Mr Goodman – the chap we used to call... er... 'Goody' – so I put this bucket of water over the classroom door but it fell on him and he got soaked, you see. Ha ha. I've never seen anyone so angry. Oh, it was a good one, that.

Presenter: Thank you very much, Jack. And now Shirley.

Shirley: Yes.

Presenter: Now, can you tell me about your first holiday away from home?

Shirley: Oh yes . . . er . . . yes . . . er . . . at the age of eight it was. We went on holiday to the Lake District. We stayed at a little guest house, just me and my parents. Er . . . I remember we had . . . er . . . honey for breakfast with . . . er . . . the toast and . . . oh . . . and porridge – I hated it.

Presenter: That sounds lovely – oh, porridge, you hated it?

Shirley: Ha ha.

Presenter: Well, what about your first day at school?

Shirley: Well, I . . . I . . . I don't remember any special incidents . . . er. . . . Oh, I was very frightened and shy at first . . . er . . . I . . . I know that, I can remember, but I soon came to enjoy school.

Presenter: So your school days, were they happy?

Shirley: Oh yes, I loved school! Oh, I was sorry when half-term came and . . . and when the holidays came. Oh, perhaps this was because I was a bit of a goody-goody.

Presenter: And what about your teachers? Did you have a favourite?

Shirley: I did, yes. I remember her well, she was called Miss Brown and she was our history teacher. Oh, she really made history come to life, she really did.

Presenter: Were there any bad moments? Did you have a worst teacher?

Shirley: Aye, I did and I can remember her name too. Her name was Mrs Sharpe and she taught maths. Oh, she had no patience. I wasn't all that good at maths and she always said to me, 'You stupid girl!' It put me off maths for life.

Presenter: Oh, what a shame.

Shirley: I know.

Presenter: Perhaps you could tell me about your last day at school?

Shirley: Oh yes, well, I'm afraid I cried. We sang our favourite hymn at the end of the term and I cried. It brought the tears to my eyes.

Presenter: Oh, and it's bringing a tear to my eye now. Thank you very much.

Shirley: Thank you.

Presenter: And thank you too, Jack Thompson, thank you very much. Next week we'll be hearing from two people who were born in 1920 and 1910. So from me, Libby Freeman, goodbye.

(Time: 3 minutes 35 seconds)

MEMORY LANE

IN GROUPS OF 3 OR 4

People with poor memories may need more reminding than others or may take longer to get started. Encourage them to keep trying! Join in by offering some of your own reminiscences.

I'LL NEVER FORGET THE DAY I . . .

ALONE first and then in GROUPS OF 3 OR 4

You may prefer to control events by issuing bits of paper to everyone, half of which say TRUTH and the other half LIE. Give these out at random.

DETECTIVE WORK

IN PAIRS

In case anyone demands the right answer to this puzzle, explain that the police are baffled and that any help in piecing together the story will be gratefully accepted by Scotland Yard, or give your own version and ask for criticisms.

LIVING IN THE PAST

IN GROUPS OF 3 OR 4

Form cross-groups for students to exchange ideas on the contents of their time capsules.

WORLD EVENTS

IN PAIRS OR GROUPS OF 3

Clues may be given to baffled pairs or groups by revealing one or two of the right answers. Here are the correct events in chronological order:

1789   Revolution in France
1815   Napoleon defeated at Waterloo (Belgium)
1848   *Communist Manifesto* published in Britain
1867   First paperback book published in Germany (*Faust I*)
1885   First petrol-driven car in Germany
1895   First cinema film in France
1900   *Interpretation of Dreams* in Austria
1921   End of civil war in Russia
1929   Depression in USA and Europe started
1942   First tape recorder in USA

1945 First atomic bomb exploded in USA (New Mexico)
1957 First space satellite launched from Russia

Make sure no one gets bogged down on the 'history test' and has time to think of the consequences of each event and time to think up 3 more world-shaking events (with or without dates).

THE WAY WE WERE

IN PAIRS

Clockwise from the top left, the photos show:
the 1930s, the 1920s, the 1950s, the 1960s, centre the 1940s.

Possibly your own memory goes back further than some of your students', so if you do remember the 50s you could tell them about life then. Or how about the 60s?

WRITTEN WORK

1 Write a story beginning 'I'll never forget the day I . . .'
2 Write a story giving your version of the events shown in 'Detective work' on page 35.
3 Can you remember what was different about life 10 years ago? Describe the differences as if you were writing to someone who has a very bad memory.

10   A night out

This unit deals with talking about entertainment, show business and restaurants.

Vocabulary

the stage
show business, play, show, musical, ballet, opera, nightclub, stage, stalls (orchestra), circle, balcony, gallery
plot, performance, script, acting, set

people
actor/actress, star, performer, dancer, singer, clown, acrobat, producer/director (director), playwright

music and musicians see Unit 8 'A quiet evening in'

the cinema
screen, cinema (movie theater), film (movie/motion picture), western, thriller, horror film, comedy, war film, cartoon
hero, heroine, villain, character, director, scriptwriter

reactions to entertainment
IT WAS . . . *good, brilliant, fine, marvellous (marvelous), magnificent, hilarious, entertaining, exciting, moving, thrilling, breathtaking, terrific, superb*
bad, awful, lousy, poor, rotten, weak, terrible, appalling, dull, boring, uninspired, disappointing, dreadful

eating see also Unit 8 'A quiet evening in'
restaurant, café, cafeteria, canteen, snack bar, pub, bar, hotel, club
menu, wine list, course, dish, helping, service charge, cover charge
cook/chef, waiter/waitress, wine waiter (wine butler), barman/barmaid (bartender)
hot/peppery, salty, spicy, sour, sweet, bitter
delicious, mouth-watering, tasty, tasteless, dull, unpleasant, disgusting

drinking
aperitif, spirits (liquor), lager – UK, bitter – UK, booze, cider, wine: sweet, dry, red, rosé, white, vintage

WHERE SHALL WE GO?

IN GROUPS OF 3 OR 4

Make sure each group decides what to do on *three* successive evenings, so that different tastes can be catered for.

The recording of snatches of overheard conversations gives the students a 'consumer guide' to some of the entertainment shown in the Entertainments Guide.

You may disagree slightly with some of the verdicts shown in the model below.

Transcript

Woman: . . . I didn't think much of it really.

Man: Why not?

Woman: Well, I mean, if I go to the theatre, I expect more than just a laugh. Or at least I want to see some actors I've heard of. I mean, have you ever heard of Peter Graves or Helen Christie?

Man: No, I don't think so.

Woman: Well then . . .

(No Sex, Please – We're British)

Man: . . . Well, it . . . it's about Mozart.
Woman: Don't you mean it's by Mozart – an opera or something?
Man: No, no, no, look: it's about a time in his life when he was the rival of
           another composer . . . er . . . in Vienna.
Woman: What was it like?
Man: Brilliant, brilliant. I mean, if you want a thought-provoking evening
           in the theatre, that's the one you want to see.
Woman: Where's it on at?
Man: Her Majesty's, you know, in the Haymarket . . .

(*Amadeus*)

First man: . . . Huh, it sounds to me just like another horror film.
Second man: Not at all, I mean it was frightening, there's no denying that, but
              it was superbly made . . . the acting was marvellous.
First man: But I don't like being frightened.
Second man: No, no, really, there was only one really frightening moment and
              everything else was sort of . . . sort of leading up to that. That was
              . . . it was . . . yeah, it was when the couple were alone together in
              this old house and . . . and suddenly . . .

(*He Knows You're Alone*)

First woman: . . . Yeah, but I don't really like musicals.
Second woman: No, neither do I normally, but Bob had already got the tickets
               and I only went along to keep him company, really. And I'd
               never been to the Victoria Palace either.
First woman: And?
Second woman: Well, it was quite entertaining. Oh, there were some lovely
               songs and the dancing was good, too.
First woman: Think I'd enjoy it?
Second woman: Well, on the whole I think you would, yeah . . .

(*God Only Knows*)

Woman: . . . I've seen both the Osborne and the Chekhov, actually.
Man: Mmm. Any good?
Woman: Not really. Oh, I mean the Osborne's quite entertaining. It's
           interesting to see it revived but I don't really think the 50s have got
           much to say to us . . . you know . . . now in the 80s. The Chekhov's
           just a bore really.
Man: Oh, they got really good reviews.
Woman: OK, it was well done I suppose, but as far as I'm concerned it's just a
           bad play.
Man: Oh, come on! I mean I remember seeing it done at the Old Vic
           in '78 . . .

(*Look Back in Anger and Three Sisters*)

Man: . . . Are you going to the Vivaldi concert at the Albert Hall?
Woman: No, who's doing it?
Man: Barenboim with the ECO – should be good.
Woman: Oh, nice! I've got their record of the Four Seasons. I think it's the best
          version there is.
Man: Like to come along, then? There are still a few seats left.
Woman: Oh yes, please, I'd love to! It sounds like a concert I really mustn't
          miss!

(*Vivaldi Concert*)

Woman: . . . I was once taken to see 'Swan Lake' when I was at school. Never
          again!
Man: But this is different, you know, this isn't 'Swan Lake'. The music's
          really lively and the dancing isn't anything like you see in 'Swan
          Lake'. Well, it's . . . it's just fun.
Woman: I'm not keen, really. I'd rather go to the pictures.
Man: Oh, come on. Don't be such a stick-in-the-mud. It's really a great
          show and you never know, it might convert you to ballet. Look, I
          promise you you'll enjoy it. I'll even buy the tickets for you.
Woman: Well, in that case, perhaps I'll come . . .

(*Façade*)

(Time: 3 minutes 10 seconds)

NIGHTLIFE

IN PAIRS

When the pairs have finished filling in the questionnaire, they should all
stand up and go round the class and try to find other students who share
some of their tastes. Encourage them to share experiences of evenings
out in the town they are studying in too.

WHAT A GREAT FILM!

IN PAIRS

When they have finished the activity and told their story to another pair,
encourage your students to tell the story of a film they have *really* seen
which impressed them.

LET'S EAT!

Get the groups to imagine that they are standing in the street and evaluating the menus outside three restaurants next door to each other. When they have decided which one to dine at, they can pretend to go in and decide which dishes to order. (Perhaps you could announce that each restaurant offers a 20% discount today to parties who order the *same* dishes from the menu – this may provoke a more animated discussion.) When they have decided what to eat they should look at the wine lists (to be found in communication activities 34, 37 and 53). At the end organise a role-play with groups taking it in turns to be diners and restaurant staff.

HOME COOKING

IN PAIRS

Arrange pairs in a multinational class so that there are a lot of bi-national restaurants. Later the pairs will explain some national dishes.

WRITTEN WORK

1   Write a recipe describing how to prepare one of your favourite dishes or a typical dish from your country or region.
2   Describe your favourite restaurant, café, bar, disco or nightclub.
3   Imagine that you want to go out to celebrate something very special, like an anniversary or a birthday or success in an exam or interview. Where are you going to go and what kind of evening are you going to have?

11 One of these days

This unit deals with talking about future events, possibility, probability and certainty.

Vocabulary

future time
one of these days, sometime soon, eventually, in the near future, in a little while, shortly, by and by, the day after tomorrow, the week after next, never

possibility, probability, certainty
perhaps, maybe, possibly, probably, definitely, certainly, surely
IT'S . . . probable, likely, possible, certain, unlikely . . . THAT . . .

plans
intentions, expectations, ambitions, hopes, aspirations, prospects, outlook, forecast, prediction

AS TIME GOES BY

IN PAIRS

A socially conscious class could be divided up into pairs or groups, each supposing that the children come from different backgrounds:
a well-off family in their country
a deprived family in their country
a well-off family in, say, the USA
a poor family in, say, India
a family in, say, the USSR

CHANGES

IN GROUPS OF 3 OR 4

The future can be a depressing prospect, but for this activity try to make everyone feel optimistic and talk about their aspirations rather than their fears.

A VISION OF THE FUTURE 📼

IN GROUPS OF 3 OR 4

In Oceania, there are three super-states, constantly at war.	**False**
Each state uses atomic weapons in its wars.	**False**
Life in Oceania is controlled by The Party.	**True**
The leader of The Party is called Winston Smith.	**False**
Most people in Oceania are not Party Members.	**True**
Every room has a small television set.	**False**
Discussion and argument is encouraged by the Thought Police.	**False**
Language is used with more precision than it is nowadays.	**False**
People in Oceania are not allowed to fall in love.	**True**
Food and drink are poor and in short supply.	**True**

Four of the ministries are the Ministry of ...*Truth*..., the Ministry of ...*Peace*..., the Ministry of ...*Plenty*..., and the Ministry of ...*Love*....
Four slogans are 'Big Brother is ...*watching you*...', 'War is ...*peace*...', 'Freedom is ...*slavery*...' and 'Ignorance is ...*strength*...'.

Transcript

Presenter: ... and the book is published by Penguin at £2.95. And now our regular look at a well-known classic. This week Elizabeth Hartley talks about George Orwell's *1984*. Elizabeth, leaving aside the literary merits of the novel for a while, can you tell us something about the kind of world Orwell shows us in the book?

Elizabeth: Well, certainly, yes, yes. You see, Orwell's world of the future is divided in ... into 3 super-states. They're called Oceania, Eurasia and Eastasia. They're engaged in a war which is waged over Africa and the Middle East and India and this war goes on for ever and has absolutely no purpose at all. Each of these 3 super-states possesses nuclear weapons but they don't dare use them.

Presenter: Uhuh. Now the hero of the book, er ... Winston Smith, lives in Oceania?

Elizabeth: Yes, he lives in Oceania, one of the 3 super-states. The Party controls every aspect of life in Oceania. Er ... the ... the leader of the Party is called Big Brother and he's worshipped by the whole population and everyone obeys him. There's a slogan that goes up everywhere and it says 'Big Brother is watching you'.

Presenter: Which has actually ... er ... come into common usage in the language: Big Brother.

Elizabeth: It has, that's right. In this society in Oceania, where Winston Smith, the hero, lives, there are si ... 3 social groups. There are the Proles –

that's 85% of the population, the Outer Party – that's 13%, and then there's the élite . . . the élite group, they're called the Inner Party and that's 2% of the population. Every room in every house in every place in Oceania has a television set in it and it's got a two-way screen. That means that . . . the people on the other end can watch the people in the rooms. Now, mindless programmes keep everyone happy. Anyone can be observed at any time by the Thought Police   you see, there's no privacy, there's no secrecy in this society. The sound of these huge television sets can be turned down, but it can never be turned off. The Thought Police punish anyone who shows any individuality or any desire to change the system.

Presenter: Mmm. Now . . . er . . . throughout the book there . . . there's a lot of talk about the various ministries of . . . of . . . er . . . the government.

Elizabeth: Yes. Yes.

Presenter: Er . . . some incredible ministries that we probably would never think of.

Elizabeth: Yes, right, the . . . er . . . the Thought Police, for example, they belong to a ministry called the Ministry of Love and their methods are torture and brainwashing. That's how they keep people in control. Language is used, not as a means of communication between people but actually to distort the truth. Yeah, you see, language is also controlled centrally. It's controlled by a ministry called the Ministry of Truth. And language, propaganda, that's their province.

Presenter: Mmm. So in fact . . . er . . . every . . . everything in a way is opposite. So the Ministry of Truth is really the ministry of lies.

Elizabeth: That's right, I mean they . . . they have slogans like 'War is peace', 'Freedom is slavery', you know, 'Ignorance is strength'. These slogans are . . . these slogans are the brainwashing methods. In this kind of society, of course, real relationships between human beings are not encouraged. So love isn't permitted at all . . .

Presenter: What, even not permitted?

Elizabeth: Oh, no, not permitted. I mean, there's no way people are allowed to form love relationships. They are allowed to have sex from time to time, but that's simply for the procreation of children.

Presenter: If they're allowed by the Ministry?

Elizabeth: If they're allowed by the Ministry. Oh, yes. Individuals have no . . . have no say in the matter. Um . . . now, food and drink . . . food and drink are controlled by a Ministry called the Ministry of Plenty. Yes, of course, the . . . the anomaly here is that food is very scarce, it's rationed and it's flavourless. There's only one brand of every product. The . . . the names are wonderful, I mean: Victory Gin, Victory Cigarettes, you know, things like that. The Ministry of Love really deals in hatred and the Ministry of Plenty deals in scarcity. Well, the Ministry of Peace is . . . well . . . well, you know, what do you think?

Presenter: Well, I've read the book so I know it's the ministry of war. But . . . er

... well, how close are we to a society like that, I wonder? Now, Elizabeth, um ... what about the style of the book?

(Time: 4 minutes 20 seconds)

THE TIME MACHINE

IN PAIRS

After a time, the pairs combine to compare notes, and then they can remain as groups of 4 to consider the problems of deciding what changes they expect to see and what they're going to do during the time they're visiting the future.

A LONG WEEKEND

IN 3 GROUPS to start with

Each group begins by looking at a different activity (13, 10 or 33) and then they 'prepare their case' for the best way to spend the weekend.
Group A want to stay in town (13).
Group B want to go to the mountains (10).
Group C want to go to the seaside (33).
When they are ready, the groups recombine as cross-groups containing one member from each of the original groups. Then the discussion begins and a compromise is reached – or total disagreement ensues.

HOW CERTAIN ARE YOU?

IN PAIRS

It might make a nice introduction to get members of the class to place bets on the likelihood of various events happening before the end of today's class. For example, that someone will sneeze before the end of the lesson; someone will apologise before the end of the lesson; or someone will use the word 'unless' in the next ten minutes.

Don't forget to return to the predictions that have been made during your lesson next week (or make it tomorrow's lesson if there is one).

PANGLOSSIA 🎭

IN 3 GROUPS

In this role simulation, each group works as a committee to consider the future of their island. Later each committee makes its report to the assembled class. (Or cross-groups, consisting of members of each committee could be formed instead.)
Committee A discuss building (15).
Committee B discuss transport (22).
Committee C discuss commerce (45).
Allow a good 20 to 30 minutes for this simulation.

('All is for the best in the best of all possible worlds' – Pangloss in Voltaire's *Candide*.)

WRITTEN WORK

1 Write a letter to a friend who is coming to see you next weekend, describing all the things you'll be able to do together.
2 What are your ambitions? Write a description of your own life as you hope it will be in ten (or twenty) years' time.
3 Imagine you have travelled in 'The time machine' on page 44 to your own town in 100 years' time. What can you see around you?

12 Home sweet home

This unit deals with talking about different kinds of houses and homes and about household furniture and equipment.

Vocabulary

houses
flat (apartment), bungalow, detached house, semi-detached house, terrace house, cottage, bed-sitter/studio flat (studio apartment)

people
resident, owner, landlord, landlady, tenant, lodger

rooms
kitchen, bedroom, hall, loft, attic, veranda (porch), balcony, terrace, living room, dining room, study (den), cellar, basement, spare room/guest room

in a living room
wallpaper, carpet, rug, mat, curtains (drapes), blind, radiator, fireplace, bookcase, coffee table, double glazing, French windows

in a bedroom
wardrobe, dressing table, double bed, single bed, twin beds, bunk beds, cot (crib), chest of drawers, cupboard (closet), sheets, blankets, pillows, quilt/duvet, bedside table

in a kitchen
sink, draining board, dishwasher, washing machine, tumble dryer, refrigerator, oven, cooker

in a bathroom
washbasin, bath (tub), shower, taps (faucets), toilet/loo/lavatory (john), bidet

outside the house
garden (yard), fence, hedge, flowerbed, lawn, greenhouse, shed

living
cosy, comfortable, homely, practical, functional, brand-new, second-hand, modern, old-fashioned, traditional, antique

THE INSIDE STORY 🔲

IN PAIRS

The missing items from the list in the Student's Book are:

2 Foldaway double bed and mattress   9 Fitted wardrobe
4 Washing machine   11 Sofa
6 Electric cooker   13 Coffee tables
8 Refrigerator   14 Roller blinds

Transcript

House agent:	... right, if you'd just come this way.
Woman:	Thank you.
Man:	Yes.
House agent:	Er ... on the right here we have the ... er ... the bathroom, which as you can see is fully ... fully fitted. If we just move forward now, we ... er ... come into the er ... main ... main bed-sitting room here. And ... er ... on the left are dining room table and chairs.
Woman:	Oh yes.
Man:	Yes.
House agent:	And er ... straight ahead of us ... um ... foldaway double bed and mattress, which I think you'll agree is quite a novel idea.
Man:	Oh yes.
House agent:	And then ... um ... to ...
Woman:	Behind the armchair.
House agent:	Yes, behind the armchair. To our right, um ... in the corner there, a fitted wardrobe. And another one on my left here.
Woman:	On either side of the bed?
House agent:	Yes, that's right. That's right, so you can put all your ... er ... night attire or what ... whatever you like in there.
Man:	Yes, that's good.
House agent:	Then, there ... the ... we have the sofa here ... er ... in front of the ... um ... the window.
Man:	Oh yes.
House agent:	Er ... so there's plenty of light coming through into the room and as you can see there's a nice view through the windows there.
Woman:	No curtains, though.
House agent:	No curtains, but we've got roller blinds.
Woman:	Oh.
House agent:	Yes, they're nice and straightforward. No problems about that – don't have to wash them of course. And ... um ... on the left of the ... er ... sofa there, you can see nice coffee tables ... er

	. . . and . . . matching with the coffee table of course in front of us.
Woman:	Oh yes, they're the same, aren't they?
House agent:	If . . . if we move straight a . . . straight ahead, actually, into the . . . er . . . the kitchen you can see that um . . . on my left here we've got a washing machine, tumble dryer and . . . um . . . electric cooker. . . .
Woman:	Oh yes.
Man:	Mmm.
House agent:	All as you can see to the most modern designs. And there um . . . on the other side of the kitchen . . . um . . . refrigerator there in the . . . in the corner.
Man:	Oh yeah, yes.
Woman:	Oh, what a nice little cubbyhole! Yes, very neat.
House agent:	Yes. Well . . . um . . . I don't know whether you've got any questions. That's it, of course.
Woman:	Well, could . . . could we perhaps see the bathroom, because we . . . we didn't see that?
House agent:	OK, yes, yes. Let's . . . um . . . let's go on out of here and . . . um . . . end up in the bathroom. . . .

(Time: 2 minutes 5 seconds)

COMMUNITIES

IN GROUPS OF 4 OR 5

Make sure that each group includes everyone's *own* home town or village in the list of different places.

PROGRESS?

IN PAIRS

Encourage everyone to try to imagine themselves in the situation.

MY DREAM HOUSE

IN GROUPS OF 3 OR 4

Make sure everyone follows the instructions and makes their choices of rooms before they start to design the building and grounds.

WHICH HOUSE?

IN PAIRS

After the activity, get each student to describe his or her own house or flat to a partner and perhaps the partner could attempt a rough sketch of the building.

WHOSE ROOM?

IN PAIRS OR GROUPS OF 3

At the end, ask each group to share their two sets of 3 adjectives with the rest of the class. Make your own suggestions and describe your own favourite room to them, perhaps.

A STUDIO FLAT

IN GROUPS OF 4 OR 5

Perhaps take a vote at the end on the best plan for converting your classroom into a bed-sitter – a large room might have split levels and quite elaborate partition walls!

WRITTEN WORK

1 Describe your dream house.
2 Describe the room you do your homework in.
3 Imagine that a friend from abroad is coming to stay with you. Describe the house or flat you live in *and* the area around it.

13 Stay well!

This unit deals with talking about keeping fit, being healthy and being ill.

Vocabulary

fitness
unfit, overweight, out of condition, out of shape, flabby, chubby, pot-bellied, putting on weight, weak
fit, slim, energetic, active, strong, muscular, athletic, agile, shapely
TO . . . lose weight, go on a diet, slim, take exercise, do exercises, jog, keep fit, go for a walk, go for a run, go for a cycle ride, play a sport

health
ill, sick, run down, unwell, dizzy, funny, well, healthy, fine, fit, better

illness
disease, infection, epidemic, flu, measles, hay fever, nervous breakdown, food poisoning, heart attack, rheumatism, backache

being ill
TO . . . cough, sneeze, sniff, groan, gasp, moan, sigh, snore, hiccup/hiccough, burp/belch, be sick, throw up, feel sick, be seasick, feel sore, feel tender, be swollen, be painful, have a temperature, feel tense

pains
pain, ache, sting, cut, graze, swelling, scratch, bite, bruise, black eye, headache, migraine, toothache

treatment
medicine for something, drug, pill, tablet, tonic, ointment, lotion, drops, injection, bandage, plaster (Bandaid)
TO . . . treat, cure, examine, diagnose, operate

people
nurse, surgeon, specialist, sister, family doctor, matron, midwife
patient, casualty, outpatient, invalid

places
hospital, clinic, ward, surgery (doctor's office), operating theatre, waiting room, ambulance

KEEPING FIT

IN PAIRS

People can easily feel embarrassed about their own physique, so make
sure that confidences are exchanged within each pair but are not
allowed to become public. Fat people in particular may easily get upset.

EXERCISES

IN GROUPS OF 3 OR 4

If we number the exercises in the first column 1 to 5 and the second 6 to
10, the actual levels are:

1 Intermediate   6 Elementary
2 Intermediate   7 Beginners
3 Elementary   8 Advanced
4 Beginners   9 Elementary
5 Advanced   10 Intermediate

DOCTOR'S ORDERS

IN PAIRS OR GROUPS OF 3

1 The people shown in the drawings have the following complaints or
   conditions:
   black eye, headache (or worry?), toothache, spots or a rash (or
   measles?), pregnancy, baldness, wasp or bee sting (different
   treatments!), pot belly.
2 Here are model answers for the listening exercise:

	Problem	Advice or treatment	?
First patient	Bad back	Rest and sleep (hard mattress)	A worrier
Second patient	Injured wrist	Go to hospital for an X-ray	Sensible man
Third patient	Smoker's cough	Give up cigarettes	Weak-willed
Fourth patient	Insomnia	Hot drink with whisky →mild sleeping pills	Nervous

Transcript

Doctor: Oh, good morning, Mrs Adams. What can I do for you?

Mrs Adams: Hallo, doctor, it's this . . . I've got a pain in my back. It's . . . it's really terrible during the day.

Doctor: Yes, does it . . . does it hurt all the time?

Mrs Adams: Well, after I've been doing the . . . you know, bending, doing the housework and then when I . . . if I stand up . . . oh, it is so painful.

Doctor: Yes, yes, let me just feel there. . . . Is that where it is?

Mrs Adams: Yes, that's it. Ooh!

Doctor: Yes, if I can just . . . I think you've strained your back, obviously, rather badly. And I advise that you have plenty of rest. Don't do any heavy lifting. Don't do any lifting at all, actually. And . . . um . . . plenty of sleep. What sort of mattress do you sleep on?

Mrs Adams: Well, we sleep on a soft mattress, of course . . . er. . . .

Doctor: Yes, well, soft mattresses are not the best sort of mattress if you suffer from bad backs.

Mrs Adams: Well, I've never had this before, you see, it's just recently come on me.

Doctor: Yes, well, if you could possibly get a harder mattress, it would be advisable.

Mrs Adams: Yes, all right.

Doctor: All right, Mrs Adams?

Mrs Adams: Thank you very much, doctor.

Doctor: Thank you very much. Could you ask the next patient to come in, please?

Mr Galway: Hallo, doctor.

Doctor: Oh hallo, Mr Galway, how are you?

Mr Galway: Well, you know, I hate to come bothering you really but . . . er . . . I was in . . . walking in the street yesterday. Well, I was hurrying really, it's my own fault, and I tripped over and trying to save myself I . . . I . . . my wrist has . . . has swollen up during the night something terrible.

Doctor: Yes, I can see that. Oh, that's very nasty.

Mr Galway: I mean, I wouldn't have come up but the wife said, 'Go . . . go and see the doctor.' Well I. . . .

Doctor: You're very wise, Mr Galway, could I just . . .

Mr Galway: Oh!

Doctor: . . . have a look? Oh, sorry. Does it hurt there?

Mr Galway: Well, it . . . it . . . just a bit, doctor, it . . .

Doctor: Yes, yes, yes, it's. . . .

Mr Galway: Oh dear! I think it's just a strain really.

Doctor: Well, I'm *not* sure and because I'm not sure I'd like to send you to the hospital for an X-ray.

Mr Galway: Oh, I don't know about going to the hospital, doctor. Does it need all that much bother?

Doctor: I think it would be wise, Mr Galway, I really do. It would be advisable.

Mr Galway:	All right, doctor, if you think so.
Doctor:	Yes, I think so.
Mr Galway:	Do I make an appointment for myself?
Doctor:	I'll make the appointment for you Mr Galway.
Mr Galway:	Oh, no, I don't want to put you to no trouble, doctor.
Doctor:	That's quite all right, that's what I'm here for.
Mr Galway:	Well, that's very nice of you.
Doctor:	Thank you very much.
Mr Galway:	Thanks again, doctor. Hope I won't see you again, if you know what I mean!
Doctor:	Ha ha. Could you ask the next patient to come in please?
Mr Galway:	I will. . . . I think you're next, gentleman there.
Mr Finch:	Yes, thank you very much.
Doctor:	Oh hallo, Mr Finch and what can I do for you?
Mr Finch:	Well it's . . . er . . . I've got this . . . I've got this terrible cough.
Doctor:	You've still got the cough?
Mr Finch:	Well, it doesn't seem to be getting any better.
Doctor:	Yes, well you know what I'm going to say, don't you, Mr Finch?
Mr Finch:	I know. I've tried. Look . . . I . . . I've tried and I've tried but I can't do it, I can't give them up.
Doctor:	Yes, I know. . . . Well, I'm afraid you have got to give them up, Mr Finch. It's the only way you're going to get rid of that cough. Now, have you got any cigarettes on you at the moment?
Mr Finch:	Er . . . yeah, yeah.
Doctor:	I expect you have, yes. Could I just have a look at the packet? Yes? What I'm going to do with this packet is just throw them in the waste-paper basket, which is exactly what you're going to have to do, Mr Finch, it's the only way.
Mr Finch:	But I . . . what . . . can't you give me something else? I mean. . . .
Doctor:	There is nothing else, it's willpower, Mr Finch.
Mr Finch:	Oh well, I su . . . I suppose you're right. I mean, I know you're right but I . . . I don't seem to be able to do anything about it, that's the only thing.
Doctor:	Well, I think you must be determined . . . more determined and really work on that for a few weeks. Thank you.
Mr Finch:	Sh . . . shall I make an appointment to see you again?
Doctor:	Um . . . make an appointment for a month's time, would you, Mr Finch? And I do hope that you'll have given up smoking by then and the cough will have gone.
Mr Finch:	Well, I shall . . . er . . . I'll try. Thank you.
Doctor:	Thank you Mr Finch. Could you ask the next patient to come in, please?
Mr Finch:	Yes, yes, fine.
Doctor:	Thank you.
Doctor:	Oh hallo, Miss Talbot, what seems to be the trouble?
Miss Talbot:	Well, doctor, I'm having trouble sleeping.
Doctor:	Yes.

Miss Talbot: I'm afraid I . . . when I fall asleep . . . er . . . at night I tend to wake up early in the morning and sometimes I don't sleep at all.

Doctor: Oh dear, no, that's not very good, is it? Well, I would rather not prescribe sleeping tablets for you at the moment, I'd rather try other ways first. Um . . . if before you go to bed you make a . . . a nice hot drink and put some whisky in it. I think that would be a good idea.

Miss Talbot: Oh . . . er . . . no, I'm sorry, no I . . . I'm afraid I won't . . . er . . . I won't drink . . . er . . . no. Something hot and milky I have tried but it's . . . er . . . it doesn't work and . . . um . . .

Doctor: I see . . . I see. Well, in that case I will prescribe some very mild sleeping pills for you.

Miss Talbot: Oh, that's wonderful, thank you.

Doctor: And if you could come back and see me in, say, a fortnight and tell me how they work. . . .

Miss Talbot: Indeed I will, thank you very much, doctor.

Doctor: Thank you very much, Miss Talbot, goodbye.

(Time: 4 minutes 30 seconds)

BETTER SAFE THAN SORRY

IN GROUPS OF 3 OR 4

Opinions are likely to differ within and between groups on the relative dangers involved.

PRINCE ALBERT WARD

IN AN EVEN NUMBER OF GROUPS OF 4 TO 6

Half the groups look at activity 4 while the other groups look at 46. A small class could be divided into just 2 groups. Those looking at activity 4 have the social worker's report on the men in Prince Albert Ward and they have to work out how the beds can be rearranged so that everyone has a *happy* stay in hospital. The others (activity 46) have the night sister's report and they have to work out how to arrange the patients' beds so that they all get a good night's *sleep*.

When this has been decided, the groups split up into pairs composed of a member of a 'daytime' group and a member of a 'night-time' group. They look together at activity 55 and have to decide on the best possible arrangement to make as many patients happy all the time, day and night. There is not necessarily a perfect solution, but the following arrangement of beds is a reasonable compromise:

FRANCIS   BASIL   ERIC   GEORGE   DAVE   ALF   CHARLIE

Allow anyone to object to this if they want!

ACCIDENT-PRONE

IN PAIRS

The original arrangement of cartoons was:

6   2   8   5   3   4   7   1

but there is a deliberate attempt to be ambiguous, I'm afraid. This means that a perfect answer shouldn't be given to the class – other arrangements may be just as logical and it's what happened *between* the scenes shown that makes sense of the story.

WRITTEN WORK

1 Write the story of Henry in 'Accident-prone' on page 53.
2 Imagine that a friend of yours has flu. Write down the advice you would give, as if you were actually speaking to him or her.
3 Write down your solution to the problem in 'Prince Albert Ward' on page 53.

14 Getting away from it all

This unit deals with talking about holidays.

Vocabulary

holidays
*package holiday, charter flight, coach tour, self-catering, self-drive,
    activity holiday, winter sunshine holiday, winter sports, sightseeing,
    boating*
*holiday (vacation), day off, leave, visit, voyage, cruise, journey,
    crossing, trip, excursion, day out, day trip*

places see also Unit 5 'In and out of town'
*hotel, guest house, bed and breakfast – UK only, motel, travel agency,
    information office*
*seaside, coast, seashore, sea, ocean, lake, bay, tide – high/low tide, sand,
    waves*
mountain, peak/summit, range, foothills, valley, gorge (canyon), cave, cliff

activities
*climb, walk, swim, sunbathe, see the sights, visit, drive, travel, stay at,
    sail, ride, waterski, ski, laze about*

people
*reception clerk (room clerk), hall porter (doorman), courier, group
    leader, guide, travel agent, tourist, holidaymaker, day tripper*

enjoyment
*enjoyable, relaxing, interesting, unusual, unspoiled, popular,
    overcrowded, isolated, miles from anywhere, remote, out-of-the-
    way, quiet, busy, commercialised, plenty to do*

SUN, SEA AND SAND

IN GROUPS OF 3 OR 4

If possible, mixed groups of men and women should be arranged to
provoke a more animated discussion.
How would everyone feel if they had to *live* in their favourite holiday
resort?

A ROOM WITH A VIEW 🔲

One member of each pair should listen out for the advantages of each hotel mentioned, while the other listens for the disadvantages. Two playings may be necessary (as suggested in the Student's Book) and first time through students can be asked just to identify which hotel each speaker is talking about.

First hotel (centre photo)
Cost: 2 weeks full board £217
Advantages: cheap, plenty of entertainment, swimming pool, close to shops and beach

Second hotel (left-hand photo)
Cost: 2 weeks half board £311
Advantages: pretty, old-fashioned style, friendly staff, nice guests, very near to sandy private beach, dancing and sports

Third hotel (right-hand photo)
Cost: 2 weeks half board £371
Advantages: comfortable, luxurious, lovely gardens and terraces, superb food, two pools

Transcript

John: ... I'm going away this summer for a fortnight ... um ... you know, somewhere nice and warm I've got a brochure here, I don't know whether you've seen it.

Barrie: Ooh, that looks grand!

John: Two weeks – very good value, for two weeks full board for £217.

Joe: Very good.

John: Lots of entertainment: there's dancing and shows and films. It's near to the shops, look, and it's ... and it's not far from the beach, it's only 300 metres from the beach. There's a swimming pool and ... er ... they do what they call buffet meals – but I'm not sure whether that's self-service or cafeteria and things like that. ...

Joe: Probably, yes.

John: But I mean it's pretty good, isn't it? £217, you can't go much wrong at that time of the year.

Barrie: No, it's very cheap, mmm.

John: You'd ... er ... you've ... um ... been away on these sort of things, haven't you?

Barrie: Oh well, yes. Last year I went to a marvellous place. Look ... um ... hang on, I've got some photos here. Here we are. ... There, it's smaller than yours but ... um ... it's prettier I think. ...

John: It's nice, isn't it? Quite nice.

Barrie: It's . . . it's . . .yes, it is small and it's a bit old-fashioned but that's what I like and it's . . . see how pretty it is: it's white with a nice tiled roof. And the staff are terribly friendly and so are the other people. I mean, you don't come across anybody that you don't get on with. And I really liked it, I mean that was how I spent most of my time. It's very quiet and isolated really. Um . . . but it's so near the beach, you see. You just come out of the door, walk through the trees and there you are. And the beach is lovely, sandy and it's private.

Joe: Very good.

Barrie: There's no swimming pool because you don't need one. Um. . . .

John: But the big question is: How much?

Barrie: Ah well, ha ha, it's more expensive than yours: £311 but that's two weeks half board, so you get bed, breakfast and evening meal.

John: Yes I know, but mine's full board!

Barrie: Oh, you don't need lunch. No, it's . . . it was lovely. . . .

John: And . . . and £100 cheaper. . . .

Barrie: And there's dancing and sports too if you want any.

Joe: Well, earlier this year we went to somewhere really lovely. Mind you, it was very expensive. Ha ha. Um . . . two weeks, half board £371.

John: Yeah.

Joe: But it's very comfortable, look.

John: Yeah?

Joe: Yes, and um . . . rather luxurious. Lovely gardens.

John: This is the one here?

Joe: Yes, that's right. You can see the gardens and the terraces. And you have your own terrace which is very nice. And . . . um . . . the food is superb. There are two swimming pools, you know.

John: Two swimming pools?

Joe: Yes. Yes, I particularly like that because I don't like swimming on the beach or in. . . .

John: You're just greedy! Ha ha.

Joe: And . . . um . . . up in the hills – you can see the hills there behind. . . .

John: Yes.

Joe: Um . . . you need a car to travel up there but it's a lovely view up there, travelling around by car.

John: Yes, that means you've got to hire a car.

Joe: Oh yes, oh yes. Yes . . . yes. . . .

John: More expense! Look, I'm trying to do this on the cheap, you know.

Joe: Ha ha. Well, it's expensive but worth every penny.

John: I guess you pay for what you get really. . . .

(Time: 3 minutes)

EVERYONE SPEAKS ENGLISH, DON'T THEY?

IN PAIRS

Clues (actually half the right answers, but not in English) are given in the communication activities. Student A looks at activity 20 while Student B looks at 41 for the clues, but please make sure they *don't* look there until they have run out of their own ideas.

The answers are, from the top:
Danish, Finnish, Dutch, Serbo-Croat, French, Polish, Swahili, Spanish, German, Portuguese, Italian, Turkish.

HAVING A LOVELY TIME!

IN PAIRS and then in GROUPS OF 4

Try to arrange an even number of groups – half working out the 'loved it' story and the other half the 'hated it'. Later the groups can be mixed up into cross-groups of 2 different 'loved it' stories and 2 different 'hated it' stories.

WHERE IN THE WORLD?

IN GROUPS OF 3 OR 4

Less knowledgeable groups could be given a list of (too many) countries from which to choose, e.g. Egypt, Italy, Nepal, Indonesia, Zambia, USA, Hong Kong, Canada, Spain, Switzerland.

The right answers are, clockwise from top left:
Miami Beach (USA); King's College, Cambridge (England); Victoria Falls (Zambia); Rio de Janeiro (Brazil); Hong Kong; Cairo (Egypt); Golden Gate Bridge, San Francisco (USA); Spanish Steps, Rome (Italy).

SOMEWHERE DIFFERENT 🔀

IN GROUPS OF 3

Student A looks at activity 23 and is told the good points of Waitangi Beach and the bad points of Porto Adriano.
Student B looks at activity 52 and is told the good side of Porto Adriano and the bad side of Albatross Island.
Student C looks at activity 36 and is informed about the nice aspects of Albatross Island and the nasty aspects of Waitangi Beach.

Between them they have to decide which of the three (imaginary) resorts to go to for their holidays.

AROUND THE WORLD

IN PAIRS OR GROUPS OF 3

Less knowledgeable students can look at activity 50, where the countries are all listed – but not in the right order.

This activity could be done as a quiz involving the whole class. To do this, give each country in the diagram a number and divide the class into teams. A team that can identify the country correctly, give the English name for one of its inhabitants and the language they speak there gets 3 points.

WRITTEN WORK

1 Describe a perfect holiday *or* a disastrous one.
2 Write a holiday brochure description of your own town or district, making it sound as attractive as possible to a tourist.
3 Describe your own favourite holiday resort or a place you dream of visiting one day.

15 Let me explain

This unit deals with explaining how things work and describing gadgets and inventions.

Vocabulary

machines
gadget, apparatus, equipment, attachment, mechanism, motor, engine, device

parts
bit, piece, spare part, thing, switch, button, knob, lever, handle, dial, needle, scale, panel, hinge, bracket, screw, nut, bolt, nail, pin, clip
fixed, attached, stuck, connected, joined

using machines
TO . . . operate, make it work, press, push, pull, lift, fold, bend, tear, cut, go round and round, go up and down, go in and out

people
inventor, mechanic, handyman/handywoman, expert, engineer

tools
screwdriver, hammer, pliers, spanner (wrench), scissors, sticky tape/Sellotape (Scotch tape), penknife

DISC v TAPE

IN PAIRS

The prices of the different pieces of video equipment are not given in the recording – it might be worth finding out current prices before the lesson starts. Here are model answers:

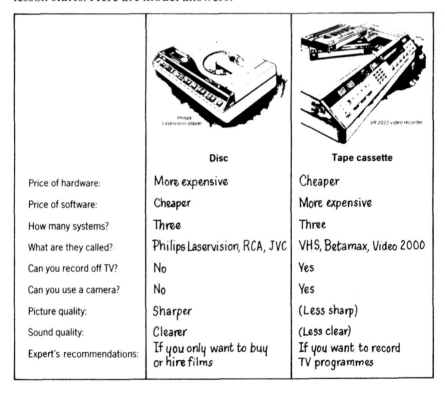

Philips
Laservision player

VR 2022 video recorder

	Disc	Tape cassette
Price of hardware:	More expensive	Cheaper
Price of software:	Cheaper	More expensive
How many systems?	Three	Three
What are they called?	Philips Laservision, RCA, JVC	VHS, Betamax, Video 2000
Can you record off TV?	No	Yes
Can you use a camera?	No	Yes
Picture quality:	Sharper	(Less sharp)
Sound quality:	Clearer	(Less clear)
Expert's recommendations:	If you only want to buy or hire films	If you want to record TV programmes

Transcript

Sally: . . . these days more and more people are investing in video equipment but there's still a problem of choice. This problem's become even greater with the introduction of disc machines as well as the well-known tape cassette machines. Alan McLean is here to give you some expert advice. Alan, first of all, what are the alternatives exactly?

Alan: Er, well, Sally, let's look first of all at the question of price which is obviously the most important to most people. Your basic machine – hardware, as we call it – um . . . the tape systems are definitely cheaper than disc machines at the moment, but of course as disc becomes more widespread, the price must drop. The software – that's . . . um . . . you know your pre-recorded films, things like that . . . er . . . discs are much cheaper than cassettes. So it's a sort of balance thing on . . . on those points. Um . . . there are several different systems . . . er . . . for disc and tape and each one isn't compatible.

Sally: Ah, tell us about this.

Alan: Um . . . disc systems: you have the Philips Laservision, the RCA and the JVC. Er . . . with domestic cassette systems, you've got the Japanese VHS system and the Betamax system. Oh, and there's the European Video 2000 . . . er . . . that's . . . er . . . another one, not perhaps as popular as the other two, but still there. There are others, but . . . er . . . those . . . those are the three important ones that you're likely to find in the shops. Um . . . you know it's difficult to weigh up because each system has its own supporters and its own merits of course.

Sally: Yes, what are the . . . er . . . main advantages and disadvantages?

Alan: Well, I suppose the main disadvantage which people would be interested in in . . . with the disc system is you can't record off the TV.

Sally: Oh, really?

Alan: You can only play the discs that you've bought or hired. Er . . . but, well of course with all the tape systems you can record TV programmes and buy films and so on already pre-recorded. Er . . . and you can use a camera and these are becoming more and more widespread to make your own programmes, you know, weddings or the . . . the family occasions or . . . or even parties. And of course you can't do that with discs.

Sally: No, I see.

Alan: Um . . . but . . . er . . . you know, why . . . why should discs . . . er . . . be developed? Well, I suppose the big advantage of discs is definitely quality. You get a much sharper picture, much clearer sound.

Sally: What do you recommend?

Alan: Well, Sally, it really depends what you want. If you want to buy or hire films you want to see at home, then the disc system is the one for you – especially if you, you know, if you like a good sound quality. On the other hand, if you just want to record . . . er . . . television programmes, like the football or whatever off the telly and watch them whatever time . . . er . . . suits you, you know using these pre-timing devices, then a VCR machine's the only one for you really.

Sally: I'm sorry, VCR?

Alan: Oh, yeah, VCR – that's more jargon – Video Cassette Recorder. You know, the tape system.

Sally: Ah, yes. Well, thanks very much, Alan.

Alan: You're welcome, Sally.

(Time: 2 minutes 45 seconds)

LIVING WITH TECHNOLOGY

The right answers for the 'household names' should present no problems, but just in case, here they are:
Singer sewing machine, Otis lift, Bell telephone, Edison gramophone and lamp, Waterman fountain pen, Dunlop tyre, Röntgen X-rays, Kellogg cornflakes, Gillette razor blade, Marconi radio, Birdseye frozen food, Biro ballpoint pen.

Some groups may need to be given clues like this when doing the second list:
'Wasn't the plane invented in nineteen o something?' or 'I have a feeling television was invented in nineteen twenty something.'

Here are the right answers in chronological order:

1885	Coca Cola	1926	Television
1899	Aspirin	1926	Talking pictures
1903	Aeroplane	1933	FM radio
1907	Electric washing machine	1937	Jet engine
1914	Tank	1948	LP record
1924	Helicopter	1968	Silicon memory chip

WHAT'S IT FOR?

IN GROUPS OF 4

Again, clues may be needed. In this case, each member of the group can be given a different clue because the right answers are hidden in the communication activities.
Invention A is in activity 44 and is a 'scholar's shoulder brace'.
Invention B is in activity 31 and is a 'rear-view mirror for ladies'.
Invention C is in activity 9 and is an 'automatic musical score page turner'.
Invention D is in activity 48 and is a 'device for waking a heavy sleeper'.
They are all real patented inventions which never succeeded commercially.

THE DOG EXERCISING MACHINE

IN GROUPS OF 3 OR 4

Here are the analyses which accompanied each invention in the book
from which they are taken – *The Dog Exercising Machine* by Edward de
Bono (Jonathan Cape 1970).

Geoffrey McGuinness

This robot has no human features at all but is just a box on wheels. Very
functional. The lead is simply hitched on to a hook instead of being clutched
in robot fingers. An 'electric signal' goes from the TV-type aerial on the
transmitter station to the TV-type aerial on the robot. Special feature of a
jumping fence which folds out in order to give the dog on the lead some
jumping exercise.

Jonathan Williams

The dog could have been attached directly to the bicycle by a lead. But
instead the attachment is through the dog's interest in the huge bone. This is
more humane since the dog can give up when his tiredness exceeds his
interest in the bone. The light on the bike is shining, otherwise there is no
point in having a light (or perhaps the dog is just being exercised in the
evening at the usual time). Bike, bone and dog are all labelled even though
they are clearly recognisable. The dog with drooping head and tail looks a bit
unhappy. The bone has the standard bone shape.

Katie Pratley

Basically a conveyor-belt but with a sophisticated temptation arrangement.
The dog thunders after the rabbit shown on the cinema screen while the
ground moves backwards beneath his feet. To increase the attraction of the
rabbit image, special rabbit smells (stored in bottles) are injected through
multiple nozzles into the exercise area. This may be a foretaste of the
'smellie' movies of the future. Separate control systems for the rabbit smells
and the film but buttons are clearly marked 'press'. Exceptional viewpoint
from above and behind. Well carried through. The tubes carrying the rabbit
smells end on one side of the walls and the nozzles appear on the other.

Anthony Butcher

A very simple design. A maze with meat (on a plate) at one end. You put the
dog in at the other end and he exercises himself in his efforts to find the way
to the meat. The maze is quite a good one and has several blind alleys. Some
of the areas are, however, unusable since they have no entrance. The
stupider the dog the more exercise he has (if not on the first occasion then
on subsequent ones).

LISTEN CAREFULLY 〔▭〕

ALONE

Make sure everyone is supplied with a piece of paper and a paper clip so that they can follow the instructions themselves. Perhaps scissors too.

Transcript

Annie: To make this you need a piece of paper about 15 cm by 10 cm. The way you make this is to cut or tear a piece of A4 paper into four.

Charles: I've got it – into four bits, right.

Annie: Right. Yes, the first thing is to fold it in half obviously. . . . Tear it down the middle. Right, now fold one of those halves again . . .

Charles: Yes.

Annie: . . . and you tear that down the middle too. And now you've got your piece of paper which is 15 by 10 cm.

Charles: Right.

Annie: Put the paper on the table in front of you with the long sides pointing down.

Charles: Yes.

Annie: And get a pencil and draw a line across the top of the paper about a quarter of the way from the top. A horizontal line. Right?

Charles: Yes.

Annie: Now you need to draw . . . to . . . to draw two more lines down from that line, dividing the bottom area into 3 equal size pieces. . . . So you've divided the bottom into thirds.

Charles: 2 . . . 3 . . . OK.

Annie: Now cut or . . . or very carefully tear up those two lines as far as the horizontal line you drew in the first place. That's right, you're going to make 3 little legs. No further than the horizontal line.

Charles: No, no.

Annie: Yes, you're now . . . now you've got 3 flaps.

Charles: Yeah.

Annie: Yes? Fold the left-hand flap out towards you, like a leg kicking out, doing a high kick. Leave the centre one pointing down, and fold the right-hand one away from you as though it's kicking backwards. . . . You fold it along the line at the top, OK? Now you pick up your paper clip, which you should have somewhere on the table.

Charles: Paper clip.

Annie: Good. And attach it to the bottom of the central flap.

Charles: The one that's pointing down?

Annie: The one that's pointing down.

Charles: Done that.

Annie: Now stand up. . . . And lift up the whole object. Hold it from the top so that all the little legs are flapping. And now. . . . Let it fall! . . . What've you got?

Charles: Oh yes! A helicopter!
Annie: Clever, isn't it?
Charles: Very.

(Time: 2 minutes 25 seconds)

USE YOUR HEAD

IN GROUPS OF 4 OR 5

Get all the equipment ready beforehand. Things like scissors and sticky tape can be shared. There is no 'perfect solution' to this problem and not all the equipment needs to be used.

One (not particularly elegant solution) is shown. The matchbox is fixed firmly onto one table with sticky tape. The pieces of paper are formed into a long channel and stuck together with sticky tape. The channel is then stuck to the top of the matchbox at one end, and to the surface of the second table at the other. The ball will then run down the channel by itself.

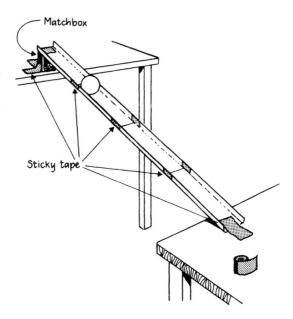

WRITTEN WORK

1 Write down your group's solution to the problem in 'Use your head' on page 61.
2 Design an invention that would make life more perfect. Give a description of how it would work, together with a diagram or sketch of it.
3 Describe a simple everyday gadget or object without mentioning its name or its function. See if your teacher can guess what it is.

16   It takes all sorts

This unit deals with talking about people, family life and relationships.

Vocabulary

people
adult/grown-up, fellow/guy/bloke, girl/lass, boy/lad, child/kid, baby, toddler, teenager, adolescent

nice
sweet, attractive, adorable, pretty, good-looking;   See also 'Nice people' on page 4 in Student's Book.

nasty
selfish, grumpy (grouchy), miserable, stupid, lazy, narrow-minded, cruel, aggressive, violent, rough, dishonest, mean, stingy, disloyal, bad-tempered, ignorant, too clever by half, crazy, cynical, prejudiced, touchy, obstinate/stubborn, arrogant, proud, rude, ruthless, greedy, jealous, nosy

neutral
absent-minded, forgetful, silly, shy, sentimental, emotional, sad, worried, nervous, scared/frightened, cheeky (fresh), naive, cunning/crafty, quiet, noisy, lonely (lonesome)

relationships
TO ... like, be fond of, be keen on, grow to like, be friends with, get to know, make friends with
dislike, hate, loathe, go off, detest, quarrel with, argue with, have a row with, fall out with
go out with (date), propose to, live with, be married to, get married to, get divorced from, be separated from, get on well with

family
cousin, niece, nephew, brother-in-law, step-father, half-sister, parent, guardian, twin, great-grandmother, boyfriend, wife, husband, fiancé/fiancée, widow, widower, lover

emotions
TO ... laugh, smile, giggle, chuckle, burst out laughing, get the joke

frown, scowl, glare, sneer, laugh at, cry, burst into tears, sigh, moan,
groan, be fed up, be depressed, feel down in the dumps (feel blue)

COUPLES

IN PAIRS OR GROUPS OF 3

In this activity students will have to make guesses – there are, of course,
no logical reasons for couples to choose each other on the basis of looks
alone.

Top row: wives 1 to 5
Bottom row: husbands A to E
The couples are as follows:
1 + C, 2 + E, 3 + B, 4 + D, 5 + A

(On page 65 in 'Happy families' there are photos of the children of each
of these couples.)

OLD FRIENDS

IN PAIRS later

The recording is in 3 parts. The first part is an example to be matched
with the first diagram in the Student's Book.
Here are model answers for the other two parts of the exercise:

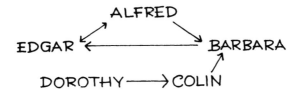

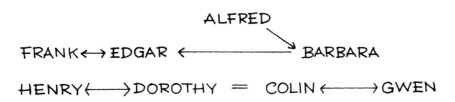

Transcript

PART ONE *(Remembering the relationship at school.)*

Frank: Do you remember Colin?

Gwen: Um . . . Colin. . . . Oh, Colin in our class at school? Oh, yes, yes, the one . . . he was . . . he was with Alfred all the time.

Frank: Yeah, that's the one, yeah. Well, believe it or not, I bumped into him the other day and we got . . . we got chatting about everyone we used to know. He seemed to have kept in touch much better than I have.

Gwen: Ah, yeah, do you remember Edgar . . . Edgar? Yeah, he was always trying to join in with what Alfred and Colin were doing, do you remember? Yes, Alfred always used to ignore him. Oh God, he used to get upset!

Frank: Yes. And then there was . . . um . . . er . . . Barbara and her best friend. Now what was her name?

Gwen: Dorothy. You mean Dorothy.

Frank: Yes, that's right, yes. They were best friends all the time they were at school. Always amused me, the idea of having best friends.

Gwen: Best friends! You know, do you remember none of us ever had best friends with anyone . . . anyone of the opposite sex? Funny, isn't it?

PART TWO *(The relationship 5 years after leaving school.)*

Frank: . . . ha ha. Do you know that . . . er . . . Colin's now mad keen on Barbara? Yes, he's . . . he's always asking her out and calling round at her place but so far she's always refused or tried to get rid of him. He won't take no for an answer though.

Gwen: Oh, poor Colin.

Frank: Yes and Barbara's still going out with Edgar, actually. But Edgar . . . well, he just doesn't seem to appreciate her. In fact, it's funny, he seems to ignore her even when they're together, but . . . er . . . well, there you go, Barbara doesn't seem to mind at all. Actually, Edgar prefers the company of Alfred now.

Gwen: Oh, he still sees Alfred?

Frank: Yeah, they seem to get on very well now. They play a lot of tennis together and . . . er . . . sometimes they go out for a drink as well.

Gwen: Mmm. So Alfred hasn't got any girlfriends, then?

Frank: Well, not exactly, no. But he . . . he does seem to have a bit of a thing about Barbara, just like Colin. But then, as I said, she's only got eyes for Edgar.

Gwen: Mmm, you know, it's funny you should talk about that, because I still see Dorothy sometimes.

Frank: Oh yes?

Gwen: You know, she told me – now, look, promise you won't tell Colin. Yeah?

Frank: OK.

Gwen: Promise! She told me she quite fancies Colin. She . . . she's dying for him to ask her out.

Frank: Well, I'm sure Colin doesn't realise that. Well, why doesn't she tell him, for goodness sake? I mean, *she* could invite *him* out, couldn't she?

Gwen: I suppose she's too shy. Now, listen, why don't *you* tell Colin next time you see him, I'm sure it won't do any harm.

Frank: Yes, but you said not to breathe a word. . . . Oh, well, let's see what happens! It might do them both good. Ha ha. OK.

Gwen: Yes, go on, yes? Ha ha.

PART THREE *(5 years later – 10 years after leaving school.)*

Gwen: Hallo, Frank. Frank! Hallo! Haven't seen you for ages.

Frank: Good heavens, Gwen! How lovely to see you. How are you getting on?

Gwen: I'm fine. How's Edgar?

Frank: Oh, very well, very well, you know, same as ever. Hey, Gwen, do you still see anything of Dorothy?

Gwen: No, no, not really. I haven't talked to her for ages really.

Frank: Oh, that's a shame. I mean, you two used to be good friends, didn't you? I . . . look, I tell you what I did hear was that she and Colin had got married. Is that true?

Gwen: Yes, yes, it's perfectly true. But actually, I . . . I think they're going to split up. Well actually I . . . well . . . they might have already. I . . . I mean, they're still officially married, they . . . they're not living together any more.

Frank: Oh, that is sad.

Gwen: Mmm, yes, you see . . . well, you see, Dorothy left Colin when Henry came back again.

Frank: Er . . . hang on, you've lost me there. Who's Henry?

Gwen: You know, Henry – Henry Bascombe, you know Mr Bascombe our old English teacher. Yes, they're living together now.

Frank: Good heavens. You seem to know a lot for someone who hasn't seen Dorothy for such a long time. Have you got . . . er . . . inside information of some kind?

Gwen: Mmm . . . suppose I have in a way . . . mmm. . . . What about the others? Do you still see anything of Alfred?

Frank: No, no, we haven't seen him for ages. Edgar . . . actually, perhaps you didn't know but Edgar had an enormous row with him a year or two back and they're not on speaking terms now. Yeah, but I still see Barbara, though. She keeps coming round to see Edgar. I don't know, but she still seems to enjoy his company, but of course he just puts up with her, not wanting to be rude or anything.

Gwen: Well, it's nice of him, you know, not to . . . but, oh it's such . . . sad, she's such an attractive girl. I'm surprised she hasn't got dozens of people hanging around.

Frank: Oh, she has. Well, one anyway.

Gwen: You don't . . . not you?

Frank: No, of course not. No, I mean Alfred, believe it or not. But she's . . . er . . . unfortunately, she's just not interested in him at all. Anyway enough about all that, what about you? Are you married or anything?

Gwen: No, not exactly, no. Soon perhaps. As soon as Colin gets his divorce.

Frank: Colin! You *are* a dark horse and no mistake. Well, I knew you must have some inside information. Cor! Ha ha.

Gwen: Ha ha.

(Time: 4 minutes 50 seconds)

FAMILY TREES

IN PAIRS

Student A looks at activity 17, while B looks at 30. Each is given a different half of the family tree of the Smith family.

After they have found out about their partner's information, they should collaborate and draw their *own* family trees and explain them to another pair.

JUDGING BY APPEARANCES

IN PAIRS OR GROUPS OF 3

Clockwise from top left: Founder of Ex-Prisoners' Society (PROP), barrister, thatcher (explain that a thatcher constructs roof coverings made of straw, reeds, etc.), careers adviser, security officer, TV documentary producer.

Perhaps write up the most useful words suggested to describe each person's personality.

WHAT ARE THEY LIKE?

IN PAIRS

Alternatively, after they have made their lists, each partner could describe just the *appearance* of each relation or acquaintance while the other listens and tries to judge his or her *attitude* to each of them.

HAPPY FAMILIES

IN GROUPS OF 3 OR 4

The children shown belong to the couples on page 62 as follows:
Sisters top left: couple 2 + E
Daughter middle top: couple 4 + D
Sister and brother top right: couple 1 + C
Brother and sister bottom left: couple 3 + B
Sisters and rabbit bottom right: couple 5 + A

When each group has made its list of the ingredients of a happy family, form cross-groups consisting of members of different groups.

WRITTEN WORK

1 Write a short description of someone you admire or like very much *and* of someone you dislike.
2 Write a description of three of the people shown in the photos on page 62 or 64. Try to imagine what kind of people they are and whether you'd get on well with them or not.
3 Describe 'the perfect teacher' *and* 'the perfect student'.

17   Back to work

This unit deals with talking about employment and careers.

Vocabulary

work
job, occupation, profession, career, trade
wages, salary, pay, income, expenses, pension

places
factory, workshop, assembly line, office, heavy industry, light industry,
service industry, headquarters/HQ, head office, branch office,
department

people
employer, employee, member of staff (staffer), manager, executive, blue-
collar worker, white-collar worker, skilled worker, shop steward,
labourer (laborer), boss, supervisor, director (vice-president),
partner, personal assistant/PA, chairman (president)

Of course, each profession has its own jargon. Try to help each member
of the class to talk about his or her work using appropriate vocabulary,
but without getting too technical.

MY LINE OF WORK

IN PAIRS

Here are very brief model answers:

His job: **Bank cashier**

What he enjoys: Dealing with
people, handling money,
responsibility, customers' trust

What he dislikes: Rudeness
from customers

Her job: **Advertising executive**

What she enjoys: Creativity

What she dislikes: Failure can
get you sacked

Her job: Doctor's receptionist   His job: Actor

What she enjoys: Five-day week, dealing with people   What he enjoys: Exciting parts, audience response

What she dislikes: Nothing really!   What he dislikes: Insecurity

Transcript

First speaker: . . . er . . . well, we don't actually open till 9.30 but . . . er . . . I mean I have to be there at 8.45 because there's lots to do beforehand. Most people think that . . . that it's just during the . . . er . . . the opening hours that we work but most of the work goes on behind the scenes or before or after opening hours. Um . . . I think what I like about it is I like meeting . . . meeting people, or rather dealing with people, because we're really stuck behind that glass thing. Um . . . we used to have microphones and used them to speak to people, but they decided it was too impersonal so they changed it back. Um . . . you know, I like dealing with people like I said, it's surprising, you know how varied the work is really. Well, a lot of it *is* routine, of course, but there's still something unexpected every day. You never know who's going to walk in and come up to your . . . er . . . position. Er . . . yeah, I do like handling money and I like the responsibility and the feeling that the customers trust you because you are dealing with their money and their livelihood. Um . . . we have our regulars . . . you . . . you build up quite a nice relationship with them. Er . . . but what I don't like is the way people can be rude or angry about little things that aren't my fault. It's usually because they've made a mistake themselves and they aren't prepared to admit it. I mean it's up to them to check if they've got enough to cover a cheque if they write it, isn't it really?

Second speaker: Well, every day is different. I mean, some days I spend hours on end meeting with clients, trying to find out exactly what they want or I try to persuade them that *our* ideas will work. Now, you see, we're very rarely given a free hand by clients. A lot of time, well yes, a lot of time is spent on research. You see, we have to do all the viewing and . . . and the readership figures. We do our own surveys to find out what a cross-section of people think. Of course it's not just what they think. I mean, people can say 'Yes, that's great. I . . . I found it really amusing and so on', but what counts is: Does it sell the

goods? Now, if we don't show a rise in sales then we lose a
client, it's as simple as that. Still, what I enjoy most is really
the creative side. Now, ideas, you know, they come to you
everywhere at the most unexpected times. In fact, the best idea
I ever had came to me when I was in the bath and I just
jumped straight out, I got on the phone to the client. You
know, I was. . . . Usually we . . . we have what we call
brainstorming sessions in the office, so the best ideas are
usually the result of teamwork. I mean, all right, we depend
on everybody being creative and this often happens best when
you're working alone, but without a good team no campaign
has a hope in hell of succeeding. *That's* what makes a good
agency – a team of individuals who can work both alone and
together. It takes a special sort of person. Now, the biggest
drawback of the work is that you stand or fall by results. If
your ideas are drying up or if you make an expensive mistake,
then you get the sack. There's always that hanging over you –
it's always worrying.

Third speaker: I'm what you might call the front man – or front woman, I
suppose. We work the normal sort of hours, you know, a
couple in the mornings and the same again in the evening. It's
only a 5-day week, which is nice. Saturdays they only see
people by appointment. Yes I enjoy most of the work
tremendously really. I like dealing with people. Some more
than others, mind you! There are the odd really difficult
characters of course. I'm known as 'the dragon' to some of
them, so I hear on the grapevine. Not that that really bothers
me, you just can't let them have their own way all the time
and some of them are never away from the place. And that can
be a bit tedious. The partners are good to work for on the
whole. There are three of them, two men and a woman. She
can be a bit of a battleaxe but I try to rise above it. I've been
with them for . . . oh, what? Oh, yes, almost 7 years now and I
still don't feel like moving on, so I suppose that says a lot for
the job really, doesn't it?

Fourth speaker: What? Well, it's such . . . such unpredictable work really. I
mean, a lot of the time you're absolutely overloaded with
work and the phone never stops ringing and other times it's
jolly hard to make ends meet. I suppose that's . . . er . . . I
suppose that's one of the reasons why we hardly ever turn
down anything. I mean you can't afford to be choosy when
there are masses of other people after the same job. . . . Of
course there are the really lucky ones who make a fortune but
they're only a small . . . small section. Most of us just do it
because . . . er . . . well, we probably couldn't do anything else
and . . . er . . . well, perhaps we've done something in our

career that's been exciting and keeps you going and
stimulating you, you know. It isn't always the money,
sometimes you do . . . a job for practically nothing, you get . . .
er . . . a great response and . . . er . . . you forget about the
money till of course the bills come in. Anyway, I suppose
that's the sort of people we are. You never know what's going
to happen. Well, I . . . I'm lucky I suppose, I've enjoyed lots of
different parts. Not . . . er . . . really rather not do the same
thing year after year after year in the . . . in the West End, but
of course if you're offered it, you take it. The worst thing? Ah,
the worst thing must really be . . . be the insecurity of it all. I
mean, you just don't know whether the next year is . . . if
you're going to get a job at all. And every time you finish a
job, that could be your last day of work.

(Time: 5 minutes 25 seconds)

JOB SATISFACTION

IN GROUPS OF 3 OR 4

Tell the class what the satisfactions and heartaches of your own job are!

FAIR PAY?

IN PAIRS OR GROUPS OF 3

If we were to include further jobs like government minister, member of
parliament, international footballer or rock star in the list, they would
all come higher than the doctor. Perhaps you could ask for comments
on this?

THE PERFECT SECRETARY

IN PAIRS

Depending on the make-up and character of your class, these pairs
could be deliberately composed of a man and a woman in each – or
some pairs of 2 men and some of 2 women. The ensuing discussion will
concentrate on sexist stereotypes and their validity.

A TYPICAL DAY

IN PAIRS

Some pairs may need some encouragement in trying to put themselves into the shoes of their chosen person, so be prepared to help and prompt if necessary. Try to make sure that within the class a range of different jobs are covered and that everyone doesn't choose the same one!

JUST THE JOB!

IN GROUPS

In this role simulation the size of your class will determine the number of groups – the main thing is to make sure that you have an *even* number of groups. Each group should consist of 2 to 4 members – ideally 3.

Allow plenty of time for this activity so that everyone has time to prepare themselves adequately for it, to carry out the interviews and then to discuss their performance afterwards.
The interview panels are likely to be asked questions about their firm: to help them to answer these, there is further information in communication activity 19. Each of the jobs advertised is fairly similar!

WRITTEN WORK

1 Describe your own typical working day.
2 Write a letter applying for one of the jobs in 'Just the job!' on page 69.
3 Describe a job you'd love to have one day *or* a job you wish you were qualified to do.

18 Here is the news

This unit deals with talking about the news media and current affairs, and describing political systems.

Vocabulary

news media
the press, the mass media, newspapers, magazines
headline, article, editorial, column, report, advertisement, cartoon strip
   (comic strip), (newscast), current affairs programme

people
journalist, reporter, correspondent, editor, newsreader (newscaster),
   eye-witness, victim, casualty, interviewer, expert

politics
communist, left-wing, socialist, social democrat, middle-of-the-road,
   liberal, conservative, right-wing, reactionary, fascist, extremist,
   moderate, radical
nationalism, patriotism, capitalism, social democracy, democracy,
   republic, monarchy, dictatorship
election, revolution, coup, majority, referendum
TO . . . be pro- . . ., be anti- . . ., vote for, elect, stand for, run for,
   demonstrate against, bring down, take over, oppose, reform

government (administration)
civil service, assembly, parliament (congress), ministry, opposition
civil servant, MP (congressman/woman), minister, prime minister,
   president
social services, finance, energy, the environment, home affairs, foreign
   affairs

war and peace
at war, at peace, army, navy, air force, armed forces
soldier, sailor, marine, officer, guerrilla, terrorist, spy, traitor, civilian,
   conscript
attack, defence, invasion, liberation, occupation, battle, sabotage,
   treason
TO . . . attack, defend, invade, liberate, occupy, fight against, spy on,
   betray, surrender

ARE THEY ALL RIGHT? 📼

IN PAIRS

Allow time before and after each part of the recording for students to
anticipate and react to the news. First of all they should read the
newspaper article together and react to that.

Transcript

PART ONE

Announcer:	. . . in Gardeners' Question Time at 2 o'clock. And now over to Gordon Chartwell in the newsroom.
Newsreader:	Here is the news, read by Gordon Chartwell. The cruise liner, Princess of Wales, which ran aground last night off the island of St Catherine in the Caribbean, is reported to be sinking. Here's a report from our correspondent in Jamaica, Graham Smith.
Graham Smith:	A weak radio signal was received here in Kingston a few hours ago from the radio operator on the 28,000 ton luxury cruise ship, Princess of Wales. According to this message, the ship is taking in water and is starting to sink. All the passengers have been ordered into the lifeboats and told to make for the nearby island of St Catherine, the coast of which is some 20 miles from the scene of the accident. In normal circumstances this would be an easy 3 hour trip, but with Hurricane Zelda approaching fast and blowing away from the island, it's feared that some boats may not make it in time to the safety of the island. Once on the island, it would be possible for passengers and crew to shelter from the wind and await rescue. The Royal Navy frigate Steadfast is heading for St Catherine at full speed but it may take her up to 24 hours to get there. So things look pretty grim for the 700 passengers and 420 crew at the moment. This is Graham Smith in Kingston, Jamaica.
Newsreader:	As soon as we have any further news we will interrupt our programmes to bring it to you. And now the rest of the news. In Liverpool today the Prime Minister said in a speech . . .

PART TWO

Announcer:	(*music*) . . . We interrupt this programme to take you over to the newsroom for a newsflash.
Newsreader:	This is Gordon Chartwell in the newsroom with a further report from our correspondent Graham Smith in Jamaica about the stranded liner, Princess of Wales.
Graham Smith:	A further signal has been picked up from the Princess of Wales within the past few minutes. According to this, the ship is now

out of danger. Apparently the damage to the liner is not as serious as was originally thought and she is still completely seaworthy and out of danger. However, before this was realised, 5 of the lifeboats had been launched and about 200 passengers and crew had made their way to the island of St Catherine where they are reported to be safe. For the time being they are likely to remain on the island. The remaining 920 people are still on board the liner and in no danger. Although Hurricane Zelda has reached the island, the wind seems to have blown itself out to some extent and although there are heavy seas, there is no danger for a ship of the size of the Princess of Wales. The ship is now clear of the rocks. The passengers and crew sheltering on the island will be brought off by the Royal Navy frigate Steadfast, which is now close to the area. Apart from a few minor injuries there are no casualties. This is Graham Smith returning you to the studio.

Newsreader: There will be a further report in our main news at one o'clock. And now back to Down Your Way . . .

(Time: 3 minutes 15 seconds)

HEADLINES

IN GROUPS OF 3 OR 4

A class who are very interested may like to spend more time on the language of headlines. Further information can be found in Michael Swan's *Practical English Usage* (OUP) under 'Newspaper Headlines', or Janice Abbott's *Meet the Press* (CUP).

EVERY PICTURE TELLS A STORY

IN GROUPS OF 3 OR PAIRS

Encourage everyone to cut some photos out of papers or magazines at home and bring them into class. They needn't be English-language papers, of course. (Possible speech bubbles for the photo at the bottom of the page might be: 'Nice looking dog you've got here!' 'No, it's a turkey, Mr President.')

I DON'T GET IT

The original captions are in activity 8. Don't let anyone look at them until they have composed their own captions for each cartoon. Point out that for 'MY SON IS INNOCENT' there is no caption, just words on the placard.

Call on your quicker-on-the-uptake students to explain the jokes to the ones who don't get them, rather than feel you have to do this yourself.

I WAS THERE

The recording is intended to be a 'starter' for the activity, hence the very straightforward task set.

Transcript

Interviewer:	Mr Williams, you were a passenger on this plane. Can you tell me what happened?
Mr Williams:	Well, basically, we were just coming in to land and . . . er . . . you know, it just didn't stop. It went through the fence onto the grass there and eventually we st . . . we did stop but, you know, there was a terrible bang and a bump and . . . er . . . it just . . . er . . . I don't know if his brakes failed.
Interviewer:	How did you feel at the time of the accident?
Mr Williams:	Well, I felt all right but a lot of people panicked, you know.
Interviewer:	Do you know how it happened?
Mr Williams:	Well, I . . . as I say, I don't know if his brakes failed or something and it . . . oh, the pilot said afterwards his . . . his reverse thrust . . . er . . . didn't work. Or was it one of the stewardesses? I can't remember.
Interviewer:	How . . . how many people were hurt?
Mr Williams:	Well, I don't think anyone was hurt badly, you know. I got a bruise on the forehead, look.
Interviewer:	Um . . . how did that happen?
Mr Williams:	Well, it was when the . . . when the thing came down with a bump all the hand luggage fell out the overhead lockers. . . .

(Time: 50 seconds)

'MAN IS BY NATURE A POLITICAL ANIMAL'

IN GROUPS OF 3 OR 4

Get everyone to make *all* their guesses before anyone looks at the right answers in communication activity 6. Afterwards perhaps you could lead a short discussion on the significance of such slogans. Can anyone think of any similar ones?

IF I RULED THE WORLD . . .

IN PAIRS OR GROUPS OF 3

It might be enjoyable and appropriate if you could play John Lennon's song 'Imagine' before, during or after this activity.
When each group has finished its list of five reforms, get them to join up to form larger groups. To stimulate further discussion, perhaps insist that each new large group has to agree on five reforms, just as the original groups or pairs did.

WRITTEN WORK

1 Write a short newspaper article (with headline) about one of the stories in 'Every picture tells a story' on page 71.
2 Write a story that followed one of the headlines on page 70.
3 Imagine you were one of the passengers on board the Princess of Wales in 'Are they all right?' on page 70. Write a letter to a friend describing your experience.

19 Atlantic crossing

This unit deals with comparing Britain with the United States and with some of the differences between the two dialects of English.

Vocabulary

typical
characteristic, conventional, average, normal (regular), unconventional, exceptional, special, unusual, hardly typical

success
famous person, well-known person, VIP, celebrity, star, superstar, hero, heroine, household name, bigwig, millionaire, self-made man/woman, (fat cat)
TO ... succeed, strike it rich, grow rich, become successful, famous, wealthy

---

A NEW WORLD 🔲

IN PAIRS

The fairly straightforward true/false questions here should present no great difficulties: this means that students can concentrate on listening to a longer-than-usual conversation for their own pleasure and interest. They can also pay attention to the accents of the two speakers, when they have answered all the questions.

In question 3 (after the listening), a multinational class could be divided up so that each pair consists of different nationalities; then, instead of imagining they're talking to an American or British person, they can tell each other about their own countries.

New York is the most dangerous city in the USA.	F
Some American accents are very difficult to understand.	T
Eating in restaurants is cheaper in London than in New York.	F
It's difficult to find accommodation with families in the USA.	F
Most Americans are helpful and friendly to strangers.	T
There are more commercials on American TV than on British TV.	T
American TV programmes are better than British ones.	F
American people apologise more than British people do.	F

British people don't show their feelings as much as Americans do.   **T**
The weather in the USA changes more than British weather does.   **T**
It's best not to travel too widely on your first visit to the USA.   **F**

Transcript

John: Yes, I'm going to the States actually . . . quite soon.
Joe: Ah.
John: Um . . . I'm a bit apprehensive about it because, you know, the stuff you
see on television makes you . . . makes me wonder, I mean, what are . . .
what are the . . . um . . . the people all like?
Joe: Well, it's nothing like the television, I can tell you that.
John: No?
Joe: No.
John: I mean, New York surely is a pretty dangerous place, isn't it? What are
the habits of people there?
Joe: Um . . . New York is not as dangerous as you might think.
John: Is that right?
Joe: Yeah, there are other cities in the States that are more dangerous.
John: Er . . . there seem to be lots of different nationalities of people there. Is
that. . . .
Joe: Oh yes . . . oh yes.
John: Is that a problem? Can you understand all different types of American
accents and everything?
Joe: Oh yes, I think if you're moving from, say, the North to the South
you're going to experience a real cultural shock as far as language is
concerned. I mean, people in the South you probably won't be able to
understand at all.
John: Is that right?
Joe: Yeah, except for Florida where . . . everybody in Florida is from New
York. Ha ha.
John: Ha ha. I see, yes. Or else they're English people going on their holidays.
Joe: That's right, on holidays!
John: What about the food? I suppose that's quite different from here, is it?
Joe: Um . . . yeah, I guess so. There's . . . um . . . first of all, there's a lot of it
. . . ha ha . . . um . . . and. . . .
John: Is it cheaper?
Joe: And I think it's cheaper, yes.
John: Really?
Joe: Yes, and you'll find . . . um . . . eating out is not as expensive as it is here
in London. I mean, it. . . .
John: Is that so?
Joe: Oh yes, yes, that was. . . .
John: Really? Do people eat out there more than they do here as a . . . as a kind
of. . . .
Joe: Oh yes, absolutely, and I think that's one reason why it's a lot cheaper. I
mean, from, you know, McDonald's to your best Chinese restaurants if

you're in New York, there's lots of variety as far as restaurants are concerned in New York and they're not expensive.

John: How about . . . um . . . you know, sort of finding places to stay . . . um . . . people's homes? Do they let them out for you to stay in? Or, you know, hotel prices, what. . . .

Joe: Oh yes, if you . . . er . . . usually if you check the papers there are a lot um . . . of places. Um . . . in New England, for instance, where people rent their homes out to . . . um . . . visitors and. . . .

John: Is that right?

Joe: Yeah, and I don't think you'll find it hard to find hotels and . . . um . . . people are generally friendly in the States about things like that . . . helping you find places.

John: Yeah . . . I'm always wary of people who, you know, sort of . . . are very open to begin with but . . . um . . . Americans. . . .

Joe: Yeah, most British people f . . . feel that way about Americans but soon you . . . I think you'll get used to it and . . . er . . . you'll find that it's genuine.

John: And . . . and . . . is the television and . . . um . . . films and stuff, is . . . is it. . . ?

Joe: Oh well, I mean, television in the States, I mean, you have here . . . um . . . the BBC with no commercials but in America, I mean, almost every television station has commercials and there's lots of them, except for. . . .

John: Yes, I don't think I'll like that.

Joe: No, I don't think you would! Although, on the other hand, I find the . . . er . . . commercials a lot more fun than the programmes! Ha ha.

John: Do you?

Joe: Yeah.

John: I mean, that's interesting. I mean, you've been over here for a . . . for a little while now and . . . um . . . how have you found . . . er . . . you know, it sounds very different in a way. There's more of everything and, you know, the . . . the entertainment and stuff. I mean, how have you found settling in here? I mean, do you find we're – although we speak the same language – very different people?

Joe: Um . . . yes. And I . . . I . . . I think . . . um . . . because there's a lot of variety in the States, for instance as far as television is concerned, you don't always get quality and that I like about a lot of television here in Britain that you get quality on the BBC. Um . . . there's a. . . .

John: Do you find us amusing? Do you think we're a funny people?

Joe: Yes. Ha ha. Um . . . um . . . yes.

John: What . . . give us an example.

Joe: Well . . . er . . . I think the way that . . . er . . . English people are always saying 'Sorry' for everything that they do. Ha ha. I think that that's. . . .

John: Ha ha. 'Sorry, I didn't quite hear what you said'!

Joe: Yes, I . . . when I first came here I . . . I had to get used to . . . er . . . people saying, 'Sorry, sorry'.

John: Does that . . . does that ever annoy you? I mean, do you find that it's sort of over-modest or something like that?

Joe: Er . . . yes, sometimes I find it so because I think people . . . it . . . it's all right to . . . um . . . be . . . um . . . a bit brassy and a bit showy about who you are. I mean, there's nothing wrong with that and I . . . I think sometimes people are very shy . . . are very very shy here and I . . . er . . . sometimes I found that difficult because . . . um . . . you know, I didn't know whether they . . . what they were feeling.

John: Yes. Do you still find there's a problem . . . er . . . I mean. . . ?

Joe: Um . . . no, once you get to know English people, I think you find out that underneath all of that it's a . . . I mean, it's just like anyone else, a lot of feeling and a lot of . . . er . . . expression, but it just doesn't always come out in public like Americans do.

John: Is there anything that you find particularly difficult to come to terms with . . . er . . . here?

Joe: The weather.

John: The weather?

Joe: Ha ha. Because it doesn't change a lot and . . . um . . . ha ha.

John: I don't know . . . I think it can change pretty. . . .

Joe: I'm always happy when the sun is shining in . . . in . . . er . . . in England. But I think you'll find a variety of weather, for instance, in . . . in the States. Um . . . you know, moving down to the South, where it's very very hot, and very very cool in the North East, you know, on the coast and you . . . um . . . the East coast is different. So you have a . . . a large variety as far as weather and . . . is concerned. But I do m . . . miss that, yeah.

John: Finally, I mean, you know, is there any sort of bit of advice you'd give me on my first trip to the States, I mean?

Joe: Well, I think the . . . um. . . . See as much as you can. I mean, the United States . . . I think the most important thing to realise in going there that it's a very large country. Um . . . I've never seen California and I'm looking forward to that and I've lived there all my life, but I've never seen California. One of the great things I'd like to do and I always advise other people to do is to ride across country because you get to see a lot of the states that way and you realise how vast the country is, how big it is.

John: And you can do that quite cheaply?

Joe: Oh yes and it's . . . it's beautiful. I've done it in parts but it's . . . it's very beautiful, it's a beautiful country.

John: Thanks, I look forward. . . .

(Time: 5 minutes 50 seconds)

TYPICAL?

IN GROUPS OF 3

This activity is supposed to encourage the critical examination of national (and possibly sexist) stereotypes and also to remind students of a variety of adjectives they can use to describe people's characters.

THE SAME LANGUAGE?

IN PAIRS OR GROUPS OF 3

Most students will need some clues to do justice to this activity. You can feed different groups different information by telling each some of the right synonyms. A class with little knowledge of the two dialects and their differences may need to be told the less obvious equivalents before they even start.
Here are the correct answers:

biscuit – cookie	full stop – period
cross – sore	ground floor – first floor
flat – apartment	holidays – vacation
furious – mad	lift – elevator
handbag – purse	motorway – freeway, highway,
mean – stingy	interstate, turnpike, expressway
nasty – mean	return ticket – round trip ticket
pavement – sidewalk	rubbish – trash, garbage
queue – line up	zip – zipper
shop – store	
sweets – candy	tick – check
tap – faucet	petrol – gas
tights – panty hose	bonnet – hood (of a car)
timetable – schedule	post – mail
trousers – pants	car park – parking lot
vest – undershirt	public toilets – rest room
underground – subway	saloon – sedan (car)
waistcoat – vest	boot – trunk (of a car)

He already did that.	He has already done that.
Did you see him yet?	Have you seen him yet?
I'm going to stay home.	I'm going to stay at home.
I'm going to meet with him tonight.	I'm going to meet him tonight.

He's gotten much taller.   He's got much taller.
I'd like to wash up.   I'd like to wash my hands.

Note that many of the so-called synonyms given above may need some
words of explanation. In many cases there may not be complete
equivalence, especially in the way the words are used. Thanks to TV
and films, most of the 'American' words given would be understood by
an educated British person, though the equivalent 'British' word might
not be understood by an American.

The final story-telling activity should involve larger groups of 4 to 6.

MY COUNTRY, RIGHT OR WRONG

IN PAIRS

A monolingual class should ignore the fourth column but still work in
pairs. The third column will still provide food for thought and points
for discussion.
Be prepared: you may be asked to provide up-to-date information about
the UK and the USA if members of the class can't do so themselves.

TOP TEN

IN PAIRS and then in GROUPS OF 4

After *very rapidly* noting down ten British and ten American household
names, the pairs join up to challenge each other and later to compare
lists. If possible, have an *even* number of pairs or include one or two
groups of 3 to ensure even numbers.

See whether the students can name the people shown in the illustration.
They are:
John McEnroe, Richard Nixon, Margaret Thatcher, The Princess of
Wales.

RAGS TO RICHES

IN PAIRS

Student A is told about Sir Freddie Laker (founder of the ex-airline Laker Airways) in activity 35.
Student B is given a potted biography of Steven Jobs (the Apple Computer millionaire) in activity 24.
If you can find out more up-to-date information about each of them, it may be interesting to see if their success has continued. The idea of the activity is for each partner to find out about the other's self-made man. Later they should tell each other about some similar men or women from their own country.

WRITTEN WORK

1 Write two paragraphs on the same topic: the first using a lot of American English words and the second using their British English equivalents. Include spelling differences if you know about these.
2 In your own experience, what are the differences between life in your country and life in Britain *or* in America?
3 Who is the most famous non-politician in your country? Write a short account of his or her life as if you were writing for a foreigner who has never heard of him or her.

20 It's only a game

This unit deals with talking about outdoor and indoor sports and games.

Vocabulary

Find out the favourite sport of each member of the class and try to offer some of the basic vocabulary required to describe it.

sportsmen and women
*athlete, player, rider, jockey, contestant, winner, loser, runner-up,
referee, umpire, supporter/fan*

sports places
field, court, pitch, course, ground, ring, rink, track, stadium

playing
TO . . . score, win, take part in, beat, draw, cheat, bet, gamble on

playing cards
*hearts, clubs, spades, diamonds; ace, king, queen, jack, joker; pack of
cards, a good hand; to deal*

playing chess and other board games
*chessmen: king, queen, bishop, knight, castle, pawn; draughts
(checkers); board, pieces, dice
It's your/my go/turn/move! Well done! Bad/hard luck! Good luck/all
the best!*

WINNING AND LOSING

IN PAIRS OR GROUPS OF 3

Make sure each pair or group spends some time discussing the role of victory or defeat in the games they play *or* enjoy watching.
How do they feel if, for example, they lose (or win) a game of cards?
Or if they come top (or bottom) in a school test or competition?

WHICH SPORT? 🔲

IN PAIRS

The sports illustrated are:
basketball, rugby football/rugger, tennis, swimming, boxing.

Transcript

First commentator: ... and McAlister bringing up the rear. And Brown is a good 4 yards ahead at the half-way mark and he's still jumping smoothly and confidently. Smith is moving up steadily, though I think he's tiring. And Brown glances back over his shoulder, he's still got a good lead. Oh, my goodness me! He's fallen, what a tragedy, he's on the ground and Smith's going past him with a smile on his face. Oh this really is a terrible disappointment for young Leroy Brown from Croydon, who had such high hopes of making the final. ...

(*Hurdling*)

Second commentator: ... backhand across court to Bradford, return across the net, Davis just reaches it at full stretch with a forehand low across the net, Bradford lobs and Davis smashes the ball into the net. Oh, what a bad mistake at this stage of the match by this 22-year-old New Zealander. ...

Umpire: Deuce.

Commentator: And Bradford serves from the left-hand court, quick passing shot from Davis who smashes that one down. ...

(*Tennis*)

Third commentator: ... and with sixty seconds left in this the final round, Robson is still very much on the attack. A left-hand jab to the shoulder has Leonard staggering back onto the ropes and Leonard is really in trouble now as Robson moves in with that lethal right hand of his, he's really punishing this 18-year-old Scot. And the referee's moving forward pushing Robson away – he's having a word with him, I think he may be going to warn him, no he's not, he's having a word with Leonard now. Leonard is shaking his head and looking terribly tired ... and the referee ... he's stopped the fight . . . it's all over and so Robson is now the new. . . .

(*Boxing*)

Fourth commentator: . . . a fine shot puts the red into the centre pocket and leaves him in a good position to take the pink and he's going to try to put it into the far pocket, he may be making a big mistake here, but Thompson is a very experienced player and he doesn't usually make mistakes. . . . Oh dear, he's pocketed the cue ball . . . a very bad error there and that really does leave it wide open for Donovan to take the frame. . . .

(*Snooker*)

Fifth commentator: . . . so it's the All Stars in the lead at the beginning of the third quarter and it's still anyone's match. Anderson with a high ball to Sampson who takes it up towards the Rochester net and passes to Green for a shot but it goes wide and the loose ball is picked up by Thomas for Rochester, across to Hunter, the 21-year-old Welsh international, who tries a long shot and it's in! 23 all now and everything to play for. . . .

(*Basketball*)

Sixth commentator: . . . Williams takes the throw and St Mary's get the ball, it goes back to Murphy and out to Green and then to Jones, who's unmarked. He's got a clear run to the far corner if. . . . Oh, he's making for the post. This could be dangerous because the Richmond fullback is gaining on him now. He looks back but he's not going to make it. He tries a kick and . . . he's just managed to make touch. Lucky there. And now there's a lineout on the far side, 20 yards from the Richmond goal line. . . .

(*Rugby football*)

Seventh commentator: . . . not a good start for the British girl but she's managing to make it up and the Russian girl is now only about five strokes ahead. And at the turn, Debbie is closing the gap, the Russian girl is visibly tiring, this is where stamina really counts and at 24 Ludmilla may well be less fit than 15-year-old Debbie Woods. And it's between the two of them, they're side by side now and with 10 yards to go . . .

what a finish! Come on Debbie, you can do it. . . .
Come on Debbie. . . .

(*Swimming*)

(Time: 2 minutes 55 seconds)

ALL SORTS OF SPORTS

IN GROUPS OF 3 OR 4

If possible, in a multinational class, arrange the groups so that each
contains a mixture of nationalities. Otherwise, if sports lovers and less
sporting students can be mingled, the discussion may be more lively.

JUST FOR FUN

IN PAIRS

Student A looks at 3, while Student B looks at 26. Each is given the
instructions for two different tricks with matches. The idea is for
students to challenge their partners to solve the problems they know the
answers to and to explain how to do them if they fail. After that they
have to solve a further problem together:
'Move 4 matches to make 10 squares'.
And here is the solution to this problem:

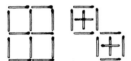

This activity may well start with little talking, but as time goes on more
and more discussion is likely to develop out of the failures to solve the
problems. Make sure time is left to do the last part of the activity where
students explain to each other some similar tricks they know.

Note: If the lack of talking worries you, you could set a rule whereby the
partner who knows the answer must not *show* the other how to do the
problem, but must *explain* how to do it.

(A supply of matches is not strictly necessary, but might be helpful if
you can find enough. Otherwise the whole activity can be done using
scrap paper, on which students draw and alter their designs.)

FISH TENNIS

IN GROUPS OF 3 OR 4

Some more sports played in or on water are:
water polo, swimming, water-skiing, windsurfing/sailboarding, diving,
scuba diving, rowing, sailing, skating (?), ice-hockey (?), curling (?).

ROUND THE WORLD

IN PAIRS

Make sure each pair has time to get involved in the imaginative exercise
before they team up with another pair.

TIME FOR A STORY?

IN GROUPS OF 4 TO 6 – each divided into 2 teams

In a small class, you might like to have 2 teams with you as referee.
Make sure that each team spends some time before the game starts
deciding how their story is going to go – point out that they may have to
modify their plans as they go along.

Here are some different endings if a second round is requested:
'. . . so we had to withdraw from the competition.'
'. . . and thanks to my skills we won the championship.'

WRITTEN WORK

1   Describe your favourite sport or game and explain why you enjoy it.
2   'Playing games is a waste of time' – give your opinions about this
    statement.
3   Describe a game you once played in or watched, beginning: 'It was a
    marvellous game. . . .'

21 Are we talking the same language?

This unit deals with talking about accents, languages, language learning and using appropriate language.

Vocabulary

language
accent (= pronunciation), dialect (= pronunciation, grammar and accent), regional accent, standard English, Received Pronunciation, variety, style, idioms, intonation, rhythm, stress, tone of voice
appropriate, inappropriate, rude, polite, over-polite, doesn't sound right, doesn't feel right, doesn't look right

language learning
TO ... memorise, understand, use, revise, make notes, repeat, practise, be rusty, make yourself understood

---

ACCENTS 🔲

IN PAIRS OR GROUPS OF 3

Make sure you allow enough time for question 2, where students are asked to discuss the accents of their own language. If it seems important, you might explain the linguistic distinction between an *accent* (a non-standard pronunciation of a language) and a *dialect* (a non-standard variety of a language with different pronunciation, grammar and vocabulary). To the layman there is often no significant difference between the two terms.

	British English	American English	Your own language
Favourite accent	Norfolk (and West Country)	Southern	
Easiest accent to do	Middle class	Standard American	
Hardest accent to do	North East – Newcastle (Geordie)	New England	
Hardest accent to understand	Scottish, especially Aberdeen	North Carolina/North of Georgia hills	

Transcript

Presenter: John, you're British, and Joe, you're American. You're both actors and in your work you both have to do a lot of different parts. Now, many of those parts require a regional accent of some sort. So, perhaps we'll start with John. John, what is your favourite accent and why?

John: I think my favourite accent is a country accent. Um . . . either Norfolk or West Country, I . . . they're the only real areas of . . . of . . . country areas of Britain that I really know.

Presenter: Would you like to give us a demonstration?

John: 'Well, I don't really know right enough whether I be . . . er . . . talking quite right, but that's what they talk like a little bit in the north of Norfolk.'

Presenter: Yes, it's a lovely . . . that's lovely. Why do you think you like this accent?

John: Because I had experience of the place when I was a child. And I think it . . . um . . . takes me back to that slower pace of life and. . . .

Presenter: Yes, very romantic, aren't you?

John: Well, far be it from me to say. Ha ha.

Presenter: Ha ha. Now what accent do you think is the one you find easiest to do and why do you find it so easy?

John: Middle class accent or anything sort of upper middle class, going up away from that, chiefly because it's the thing that's closest to me, I suppose.

Presenter: Of course. Would you like to demonstrate that?

John: 'Well, I don't know whether I'd like to demonstrate it. I'll . . . suppose I'll perform it for you.'

Presenter: That's 'really rather upper class', isn't it? Yes, OK, thanks very much. Now, what . . . what accent do you find the most difficult to do?

John: Yes . . . er . . . the Geordie accent, that's the accent North East of England . . . um . . .

Presenter: Round Newcastle.

John: Around Newcastle, yeah, that . . . that area.

Presenter: Yes, very hard, isn't it? And . . . um . . . what accent do you find hardest to understand?

John: Well, I do find that one pretty difficult sometimes . . . um . . . I think there are many . . . um . . . Scottish – and some Irish ones – but there are . . . there's the Aberdeen accent. . . .

Presenter: That's a difficult one.

John: I think some of those are very difficult.

Presenter: Well, thanks very much. Now we'll go to Joe. So, Joe, as I said before you're American.

Joe: Yes.

Presenter: Well, what's your favourite accent and why?

Joe: Well, I think my favourite accent is the Southern accent. And I think because . . . um . . . I love the music in the accent . . . um . . . the lilt, the rise and fall.

Presenter: Could we hear a bit of it?
Joe: Well, 'I think if you are talking Southern, you . . . er . . . always feel a
           bit like there's sunshine around you all the time.'
Presenter: Oh, that's lovely! Um . . . and which accent do you find easiest to do
           and why?
Joe: Well, I think probably the easiest . . . er . . . accent to do is Standard
           American because that's required most in the theatre. Um . . . it's
           sort of like . . . um . . . what you hear . . . er . . . in a typical American
           news broadcaster sound.
Presenter: C . . . could I hear some?
Joe: Well, 'it's very um . . . definite and you make sure that all of the
           words are evenly distributed throughout your sentences and you
           make sure that if you have any kind of word that has an "r" in it,
           like "better", er . . . there'll be . . . um . . . you make sure that you
           sound those "r" sounds.'
Presenter: At the end of the word?
Joe: At the end of the word, yeah.
Presenter: Right, thank you. And what accent do you find hardest to do?
Joe: I think probably . . . um . . . the New England accent . . . um . . .
           Boston and further up the East Coast, particularly when you get to
           Maine. It's a very particular kind of accent . . . er . . . I think
           probably you would have heard it most if you remember President
           Kennedy. Er . . . he took . . . er . . . pains not to . . . um . . . sound like
           that always but I think you . . . er . . . I think that's the hardest to do.
Presenter: I see and what . . . what's the one that you find hardest even to
           understand?
Joe: Well, now there's a particular accent in the hills of . . . um . . . North
           Carolina and the North of Georgia . . . um . . . that's very very hard
           . . . um . . . to understand because it's very rapid. It's Southern but
           it's very very rapid and . . . er . . . it is reported that there are even . . .
           er . . . traces of Old English in this . . . er . . . accent and I . . . I find
           that very hard to understand.
Presenter: Right. That's fascinating. Thank you very much, both of you.

(Time: 4 minutes 25 seconds)

IDIOMS

IN PAIRS OR GROUPS OF 3

Don't spend too long on the first part of this activity – get students to
pick out the idioms that are particularly amusing or interesting and to
make comments on them. (The idioms are explained in activity 32.)

Students often get bees in their bonnets about learning English idioms.
It may be worth pointing out that:

a) Native speakers of English don't *expect* foreigners to use idioms –
   indeed, they may even find it amusing if they do.
b) Idioms are very difficult to use in *exactly* the right situations without
   sounding funny.
c) Your students should be able to *understand* the most common ones
   but not necessarily learn to use them too.

THE COMMONWEALTH

IN GROUPS OF 3 OR 4

The countries shown on the map are, in descending order of population:
India, Bangladesh, Nigeria, UK, Canada, Kenya, Australia, Zimbabwe,
Hong Kong, New Zealand, Singapore, Jamaica, Bahamas.

The top 12 world languages in 1981 were, in millions of native speakers:

Mandarin	713	Bengali	148
English	391	Portuguese	148
Russian	270	German	119
Spanish	251	Japanese	118
Hindi	245	Malay-Indonesian	112
Arabic	151	French	105

FOREIGN LANGUAGES 🔊

IN GROUPS OF 3 OR 4

In a mainly monolingual class each group should look at activity 51.
In a multilingual class each group should look at activity 40 and, if
possible, arrange the groups so that each contains at least two
different nationalities.

In this activity, different sets of questions are given for discussion,
giving both types of class plenty to talk about. If you have a class
composed almost entirely of speakers of the same language with only a
few others, then different groups can look at 40 or 51, depending on
their make-up.

WHAT'S IT ALL ABOUT? 📼

IN PAIRS

	Speaker A	Topic or purpose of conversation	Speaker B
1	Shop assistant	Trying to get a refund	Customer
2	Former pupil (Watkins)	Trying to get Mr T to remember him	Schoolmaster (Mr. Thompson)
3	Mother	Trying to persuade her to eat	Daughter
4	Spy	Arranging meeting and signal	Spy
5	Student who has done right homework	Homework	Student who has done wrong homework
6	Male stranger	Trying to pick her up (or just being friendly?)	Woman in café
7	Sympathetic colleague	Interview or exam	Worried colleague

Transcript

Assistant: Well, I'm sorry, madam, there's nothing I can do. The manager's out just now . . . he's the only one who can authorise it.

Customer: All right, just give me a credit note then.

Assistant: I'm sorry, the only thing I can do is let you exchange it for something else of the same price. How about that? Otherwise, you'll have to come back next Monday and see the manager. I'm sure he'll be able to let you. . . .

Customer: Oh goodness, I don't know what to do. I'm only here on a visit and I'll be back home next week. . . . Just a minute, what about if . . . if you. . . .

Young man: Well, well, well, if it isn't Mr Thompson!

Older man: Ah . . . ah . . . I'm not sure that I. . . .

Young man: Oh come on, Mr Thompson, surely you remember?

Older man: No, I'm afraid I. . . .

Young man: 1973? 4B?

Older man: Uh? Oh! 4B, let me see, ah yes. Young Watson, how are you, my boy?

Young man: No, no, it's Watkins, actually. Bill Watkins.

Older man: William Watson. Ah, you were the one who was expelled for. . . .

Young man: No, no, no I'm Watkins. Watson wasn't even in my form.
Older man: Watkins. Watkins. No, no, I'm sorry I don't know anyone. . . .

Mum: Eat it up!
Girl: Shan't.
Mum: Eat it up this minute or you really will be in trouble.
Girl: Eat it up yourself.
Mum: Now look here, young lady, if you don't do what I say, I'll. . . .
Girl: If I do eat it up, I'll be sick. Then I'll probably die and then you'll be sorry.
Mum: All right, I'll eat it myself. Mmm, it's delicious!
Girl: No, it's mine! I want it!

Spy 1: Same time next week, then.
Spy 2: Fine, and in the meanwhile I'll take care of things here.
Spy 1: Right. And if there's any trouble, let me know in the usual way.
Spy 2: OK then. Goodbye. . . . Oh, just a minute, I've been thinking.
Spy 1: What?
Spy 2: Look, I think we've got to change the signal. There's been a man hanging around outside my place and he could be on the other side.
Spy 1: All right. Make a yellow chalk mark at shoulder height on the north wall if you need to contact me earlier.
Spy 2: North wall, right. If everything's OK, I'll leave the usual mark on the south wall.
Spy 1: Good.
Spy 2: See you next week, then. And good luck!

Girl: Finished yet?
Boy: No.
Girl: Going to take long?
Boy: Don't know.
Girl: Want any help?
Boy: No, not really. . . . Listen, why don't you get on with your own?
Girl: Finished ages ago. Dead easy. Specially page 43.
Boy: 43, don't you mean 143?
Girl: No 43. Why, have you been doing 143?
Boy: Yeah, I thought that's what she said.
Girl: No, course not!
Boy: Huh, I thought it was a bit difficult!

Man: Ah . . . is this seat free?
Woman: Yeah, there's no charge!
Man: I mean, can I sit here?
Woman: I expect so, it's a free country.
Man: Thanks. It's a lovely day, isn't it?
Woman: No, not really, too dry.
Man: Yes, I see what you mean. It is very dry. Um . . . is the coffee any good here?

Woman: It's all right, yeah.
Man: Er, Miss! Coffee please. . . . Make that two coffees! Oh, are you. . . ?
Woman: Yeah, bye.
Man: Oh, but I've just ordered. . . .

Woman: How did you get on?
Man: Not very well, I'm afraid.
Woman: Oh dear, what went wrong?
Man: Oh, you know. Usual thing. I lost my nerve and went all to pieces.
Woman: Yes, but surely they must have realised you felt like that and made
        allowances. I mean everyone has butterflies in that situation.
Man: Maybe, but from the way he looked at me I could tell he thought I
        was some sort of idiot.
Woman: How did you get on with the photograph?
Man: Oh, that was easy. It was the reading that let me down, I couldn't
        make head or tail of it.
Woman: Oh don't worry. As long as you did all right in the other parts, you
        probably managed to. . . .

(Time: 4 minutes 20 seconds)

'HI!' 'GOOD MORNING'

IN GROUPS OF 3

In this activity students will be talking about appropriacy and
considering different ways of saying the same things. Here are some
ideas for sentences that will fit in the chart:

I'd like to have it. Let me have it. Please may I have it? Would you mind giving it to me? Could I possibly have it?	Hallo there. Nice to see you. Pleased to meet you. Good to see you again. How do you do.
Ta. Cheers. Lovely. You're very kind. You've been most kind. I'd like to thank you. I'm very grateful.	Cheers. Cheerio. Bye for now. So long. Be seeing you. All the best. Well, I'd better be off now.

Perhaps point out that there are no clear-cut distinctions between what is appropriate and what is inappropriate. The kind of language we use depends on the *total* situation. For more information and a great deal of practice on using English appropriately, see *Functions of English* (CUP 1981) or *Functions of American English* (CUP 1983).

YOU CAN'T SAY THAT!

IN GROUPS OF 3

More plausible sentences in this exercise might be:

Can I help you?
IPSWICH COUPLE'S £10,000 POOLS WIN
Perhaps I haven't made myself quite clear. Sorry.
In case of fire, close all windows and go to fire exit.
Help!!!
Anything to declare?
Fine, thanks very much. We'll let you know.
Second class return to Gloucester please.
What a nice jumper! Where did you get it?
And what are you going to be when you grow up?

Note that the above are not 'correct solutions' – your students' own suggestions are likely to be just as 'good' and probably more amusing.

WRITTEN WORK

1 Explain what aspects of your English you'd still like to improve. What do you propose to do about this?
2 Write a letter to a foreign friend who says that he or she is going to start learning your language.
3 'If only we all spoke the same language!' Do you think there will ever be just one world language? What would be different about the world if there were?

22 The persuaders

This unit deals with talking about advertisements and advertising.

Vocabulary

advertising
marketing, sales, public relations
advertisement, ad, commercial, poster, slogan, campaign, brochure,
leaflet, catalogue, handout

reactions to advertisements
effective, striking, attractive, appealing, amusing, professional
acceptable, so-so, not bad, nothing to write home about, amateurish,
dreadful, insulting, shouldn't be allowed

COME FLY WITH ME

IN PAIRS OR GROUPS OF 3

If possible, **before this lesson**, ask everyone to bring with them one good
and one bad advertisement from a magazine or newspaper. These can
then be compared with the advertisements in the Student's Book and be
a personal contribution to the lesson. Or, perhaps, bring in some ads
you have selected yourself.

YOUR FRIENDLY STATION 📼

IN PAIRS OR ALONE

Model answers:

	Name of company or product	Type of product or service
1	Acme Motors	Second-hand cars
2	Britannia Carpets	Carpets
3	Photofast	1-hour developing and printing
4	Colorado	Do-it-yourself store
5	New Nills	Anti-cold remedy
6	La Bella Italia	Restaurant

Transcript

Salesman: A lovely motor, squire. Look it over: only 6,000 miles on the clock, lovely body and just one careful lady owner. A real bargain, sir. How about a spin in her to help you decide?

Announcer: Don't trust to luck. Come to a firm you can trust – Acme Motors. We've been providing an efficient and reliable service to the public for over 35 years. Acme Motors on the London Road roundabout. Come and see our wide range of quality used cars, each one with a no-quibble 6 month warranty. Or if you prefer, give us a ring on 219129 or see our full page ad in Friday's Evening Post. Acme Motors for quality and service at a price you can afford.

Salesman: Looking for a new carpet? Britannia Carpets have the largest selection in town at the most competitive prices. 100% pure wool Berber at £6.99 a square metre. Genuine Axminster at £5.99 a square metre. And hundreds more bargains. Free fitting and professional advice. Come and look round without any obligation. Britannia Carpets, 101 Eastgate – late shopping till 8 on Thursdays.

Man: Bring your colour films to Photofast. We don't offer a 24-hour service, we don't offer a same day service, we offer a one hour service. Yes we'll have your film developed and printed in just one hour.

Woman: How is that possible?

Man: Thanks to our computerised photoprocessor on the premises we can give you quality prints in one hour.

Woman: Where's the catch?

Man: There's no catch. You don't pay a penny more than you would at any other photo shop in town and we guarantee that if you are in any way dissatisfied with our quality, we'll refund the cost of your film.

Woman: Where is Photofast?

Man: Right in the centre of town at 99 Eastgate, right next door to Britannia Carpets. And we're open from 8.30 to 6, Monday to Saturday. Photofast, 99 Eastgate.

Voice: Colorado . . . Colorado . . . Colorado.

Man: Colorado DIY Centre now open on Sundays from 10 to 5.

Woman: Come to Colorado for the keenest prices in all home improvement goods, gardening needs and kitchen furniture. Colorado DIY Centre in Western Avenue, next to Sainsbury's.

Man: For do-it-yourself, come to Colorado!

Voice: Colorado . . . Colorado . . . Colorado.

Girl: Oh, Mum, I can't go out this evening, I've got such a bad cold.

Mum: Come on, Sharon, you know you've been looking forward to it all week.

Girl: No, Mum, I'd better stay at home and watch telly or something. Bruce won't want to dance with me if I sound like this.

Mum: Oh, Sharon. Why don't you try one of these: New Nills.

Girl: Dew Dills?

Mum: Yes, just pop one of these in your mouth and it'll clear your head like magic.

Girl: Mmm. It tastes nice . . . what did you say they were called?

Mum: New Nills – they're 50p a packet from any chemist's.

Girl: Hmm, New Nills – they do work like magic. Well, I'd better not keep Bruce waiting. Don't wait up for me Mum. I may be late back.

Man: Let's eat out for a change, dear.

Woman: Good idea. Someone else can do the washing-up. But where shall we go?

Man: Tom at work told me about that new place – La Bella Italia.

Woman: La Bella Italia?

Man: That's right, they've just opened at 45 High Street. Their pizzas and pasta dishes are supposed to be out of this world.

Woman: Mmm! Sounds marvellous.

Announcer: La Bella Italia, for the best of Italian food and the friendliest service at a price you can afford. We serve the best pizzas in town. Try our seafood salad and our homemade icecream – or just drop in for a capuccino and a cake while you're shopping. La Bella Italia at 45 High Street. For reservations phone Mario on 519968.

(Time: 4 minutes)

AN IDEAL GIFT [⊠]

IN PAIRS and then in larger groups

Each pair chooses a present from the four shown and finds out more about it in the communication activities (activity 2, 18, 25 or 54). Then the pairs combine with two or three other pairs to try to 'sell' them their gift.

You may like to control the choices, so that everyone chooses different things. You could also form cross-groups later, so that each larger group consists of one member of each pair.

IMAGES

IN PAIRS OR GROUPS OF 3 OR 4

Don't allow anyone to look at the 'answers' in activity 49 until they
have fully discussed each advertisement.
(Dunlopillo make beds, mattresses and pillows.)

BRAINSTORMING

IN GROUPS OF 4 OR 5

Perhaps each group could be given a different product to deal with.

BOOK OF THE YEAR??

IN PAIRS OR GROUPS OF 3

Award a small prize to the winners of the contest: perhaps some sweets
or chocolates that can be shared with the losers. (The winning entries
could be sent to me c/o Cambridge University Press, perhaps.)

WRITTEN WORK

1 Describe your favourite advertisement and explain why you like it.
2 Write a 'blurb' for the ideal text book you'd like to use after you've
   finished using *Ideas*.
3 Explain what you've learnt and how much your English has
   improved after using *Ideas*. What were the drawbacks and
   advantages of the book and the way you used it?

Key to communication activities in Student's Book

Details of each activity are given in the relevant teaching notes for each unit in this book.

Unit No.	Activity title	Communication activities			
3	Oh to be in England	A: 14	B: 27		
4	On the phone	A: 12 → 43	B: 56 → 38		
5	Where is. . . ?	A: 11	B: 39		
5	A day in London	A: 5	B: 28		
6	100 years	A: 7	B: 47		
7	It's the only way to travel	A: 1	B: 21	C: 42	
7	Let's go!	A: 16	B: 29		
10	Let's eat!	A: 37	B: 34	C: 53	
11	A long weekend	A: 13	B: 10	C: 33	
11	Panglossia	A: 15	B: 22	C: 45	
13	Prince Albert Ward	A: 4 → 55	B: 46 → 55		
14	Everyone speaks English, don't they?	A: 20*	B: 41*		
14	Somewhere different	A: 23	B: 52	C: 36	
14	Around the world	50*			
15	What's it for?	A: 9*	B: 31*	C: 44*	D: 48*
16	Family trees	A: 17	B: 30		
17	Just the job!	B: 19			
18	I don't get it	8*			
18	'Man is by nature a political animal'	6*			
19	Rags to riches	A: 24	B: 35		
20	Just for fun	A: 3	B: 26		
21	Idioms	32*			
21	Foreign languages	51 or 40			
22	An ideal gift	A: 2	B: 18	C: 25	D: 54
22	Images	49*			

* The activities shown with asterisks are clues or keys to the activity in the main part of the book, not self-contained exercises.